
Imagination and Proof

THE ANTHROPOLOGY OF FORM AND MEANING

Senior Editor
J. David Sapir (University of Virginia)

Associate Editors
Ellen B. Basso (University of Arizona)
J. Christopher Crocker (University of Virginia)
Hildred Geertz (Princeton University)
Peter A. Metcalf (University of Virginia)
Renato A. Rosaldo (Stanford University)

IMAGINATION AND PROOF

Selected Essays of A. M. Hocart

EDITED AND WITH AN INTRODUCTION BY
Rodney Needham

The University of Arizona Press
Tucson

THE UNIVERSITY OF ARIZONA PRESS

This book was set in 10/12 Linotron 202 Bembo.
Manufactured in the U.S.A.

Library of Congress Cataloging-in-Publication Data

Hocart, A. M. (Arthur Maurice), 1884–1939.
Imagination and proof.

(The Anthropology of form and meaning)
Bibliography: p.
Includes index.
1. Anthropology—Methodology. I. Needham, Rodney.
II. Title. III. Series.
GN33.H55 1987 306 86–27248

ISBN 0-8165-1007-5 (alk. paper)

British Library Cataloging in Publication data are available.

This edition is dedicated to the memory of

the late Fitzroy Richard
4th Baron Raglan

in recognition of his selfless devotion to
the work and renown of A. M. Hocart

Contents

Acknowledgments

The editor and the publishers are obliged to the Archaeological Commissioner for Sri Lanka, in respect of the former *Ceylon Journal of Science*, and to the editors of *Acta Orientalia*, *Anthropos*, and *Folk-lore* for their kind permissions to reprint the articles that make up the chapters in this volume. The bibliographical particulars are cited with the respective chapters.

The portrait of Hocart that appears as frontispiece is reproduced by permission of the Royal Anthropological Institute of Great Britain and Ireland, London, and through the good offices of Miss B. J. Kirkpatrick, Librarian.

Much gratitude is due, for the sake of Hocart's reputation and on other counts, to Dr. Gillian Feeley-Harnik of The Johns Hopkins University, whose crucial aid led to the present publication, and to Dr. David Sapir of the University of Virginia and his assistant editors for the favor of its inclusion in the present series.

A. M. Hocart

Editor's Introduction

Imagination must always keep ahead of proof, as an advanced detachment to spy out the land.

HOCART

There are men whose plangent minds call to us like sirens. Their sudden thoughts pierce through the press and distraction of ordinary concerns, give a surer sense of direction, and turn us into more rapid and exhilarating courses. Archilochos was one, Sir Thomas Browne another; Hume had that nature, and Lichtenberg too. Graphically, Klee belonged to their company; harmonically, Stravinsky. They can leave us stranded in the end, or wallowing again tediously in doldrums of the spirit, yet for a time at least they promise not only security but life. It is a measure of their address that we gratefully recall only the confident hopes into which they lured us, and are not willing to account these afterwards as mere delusions. There are greater and more minor possessors of this gift, but whatever their several capacities the quality is unmistakable. Hocart had something of that character.

He was born in Brussels in 1883, of a family stemming from France, and was educated in Guernsey and at the University of Oxford. After taking a degree in classical studies he aided W. H. R. Rivers in ethnographical research in the Solomon Islands, became headmaster of a Fijian school, and then returned to Oxford before fighting as an infantry captain in France in World War I. After the war he was appointed Archaeological Commissioner in Ceylon, a post he held until his retirement by reason of ill health in 1929. For some time he worked at University College London, in association with G. Elliot Smith and W. J. Perry, until in 1934 he was elected to the chair of sociology at Cairo in succession to E. E. Evans-Pritchard. He contracted an infection while working in upper Egypt, and died in 1939 at the age of fifty-five.[1]

During his lifetime he was much neglected by the academic profession, and it was the late Lord Raglan who first and most substantially gave Hocart's works a consolidated prominence. He placed unpublished articles in journals, wrote a preface to the English edition of *Les Castes,*[2] brought out a collection of Hocart's papers as *The Life-giving Myth,*[3] edited the unpublished manuscript of *The Northern States of Fiji,*[4] and made up into a book, under the title *Social Origins,*[5] a further body of manuscripts. These admirably selfless undertakings, which had the main effect in giving Hocart a posthumous and wider reputation, were complemented by a series of appreciative citations by Claude Lévi-Strauss, from 1949 onward, and then by Louis Dumont.[6] In 1967 Fortes handsomely paid tribute to him as "that neglected pioneer," and generously recognized Hocart as having anticipated him in his own conclusions on the comparative analysis of installation ceremonies.[7] Since then, a number of Hocart's books have been reprinted in close succession: *Caste* in 1968,[8] *Kingship* in 1969,[9] *The Life-giving Myth* in 1970,[10] and *Kings and Councillors* in the same year.[11]

The present volume is a collection of previously published papers and other items, brought together under a newly devised title taken from Hocart's first book,[12] and is intended as a concluding homage under the present editorship. While not purporting to exhaust the many kinds of interest that are yet to be discerned in Hocart's scattered writings, it presents a compendium of such of his essays and printed notes as seem to have an outstanding claim to a renewed attention.

Two of the essays, presented here as Chapters 1 and 7, have been reprinted elsewhere, and a brief accounting should be given in explanation of their appearance here.

"Evidence in Human History" (Chapter 1) was used by Hocart, under the heading "Rules of Evidence," as the opening chapter in his *Kings and Councillors*. He made some small deletions and other alterations for the purpose, but it is not these minor disparities alone that justify its presence in this collection. The initial reason for its inclusion is that it has a singular importance for the understanding of Hocart's characteristic approach. It does not state merely his rules of evidence for a particular investigation, such as that into the ritual origins of government, but it sets out far more generally certain methodological precepts by which he is constantly guided throughout his writings. The precepts are, in the first place, premises that are crucial in coming to terms with Hocart's work; they are also cogent injunctions to any investigator who would try to analyze the forms of civilization. Social anthropology in particular, during the past fifty years of its modern development, has been much influenced by the ambition to emulate the procedures of the exact sciences, and this impulsion has encouraged conceptions of evidence and analysis which, according to Hocart, are ill founded.

After some of the theoretical excesses of diffusionism, and then more especially the dogmatic derogation of cultural history on the part of A. R. Radcliffe-Brown, the practice of conjecture and comparative inference fell into disrepute; with the prosecution of intensive field research the solid results of direct observation gave a new promise to the subject. It was, therefore, understandable enough that direct evidence should be thought necessarily better than circumstantial. Concomitantly, functionalism undermined faith in the comparison of far-flung institutions, and the ethnographical ideal entailed a concentration on the contemporary workings of individual societies. The patent advantages of this change of method conduced to the idea that historical comparison had been superseded in a new advance toward true science. The conjoined doctrines of direct evidence and functional analysis were thus triumphantly dominant in 1933, when Hocart leveled his critique against these tenets, and they have in the main prevailed into current views on the right nature of anthropology.

Today, Hocart's adjurations retain still their proper force, for they express points of view that are of constant value and are not restricted in their application to any particular state or period in the fluctuation of academic fashion. There is a salutary quality to his contentions that the exact sciences themselves rely greatly on circumstantial evidence, that direct evidence may turn out not to be direct after all and may not only fail to explain but even suggest a wrong explanation, and that comparative evidence alone can decide an issue. And then there is the undoctrinaire sanity and good sense of his working rule that in any case the best procedure is "not to argue about principles, not to insist that there is only one method in all science, but to get down to work," and to show by example the merits and results of whatever approach is in question. These are lessons that can hardly be too often repeated.

There is another reason to include "Evidence in Human History," and that is to introduce readers to the argument of *Kings and Councillors,* a work which can be estimated as Hocart's most mature and best integrated exposition of his distinctive interests and style of thought. A monograph on "the comparative anatomy of human society" (the subtitle), or on the original quest of life, or on the development of government—as that book may be variously received—may not at first seem to proffer so much more as is in fact to be found in it. But anyone who is taken by the kind of argument deployed in the essay on evidence, and is attracted by the freshness of expression with which it is stated, may well be gratefully induced to proceed thence to the major exhibition of those virtues.

This, too, is the chief reason for including "The Basis of Caste" (Chapter 7). Hocart's monograph on caste[13] has attracted repeated commendation on the part of experts such as Dumont[14] and Pocock,[15] and the reissue of the English edition of that work has additionally confirmed its value. In this case also, those who have no great prior interest in caste or India, or in the sociological and political issues posed by the study of these topics, may yet be led by this brief portion of Hocart's opening arguments on the comparative study of caste[16] to turn to the book. As it stands, moreover, the essay has in itself an intrinsic intellectual appeal, and it gives also a good impression of Hocart's trenchant approach to a very recalcitrant and intriguing object of study.

The selection of the rest of the essays calls for no such special justification, and only a few comments on them are called for by way of introduction. Not that there is any need simply to restate their arguments, or to stress in advance their peculiar emphases, but some more incidental observations may serve to convey an idea of their later development and present relevance.

The essay on convergence (Chapter 2) tackles an issue of the very greatest importance in humane studies, namely the explanation of similarities among customs. The two chief interpretations of like institutions in unlike and often far-separated societies have been that the similarities either had a common origin or were independent creations. A third possibility—that customs or ideas which previously were different might have converged into an identical type—has received far less attention. Hocart presents a clear case for this process by reference to language, architecture, and feudalism; but underlying these particular demonstrations, as usual, is a more general point of method. Historical changes, whether divergent or convergent, call into question the anthropological addiction to definitions. The result of this predilection is, he maintains, "to bring together those things which are historically unconnected, and keep apart those things which are closely related." And, he continues, "there is nothing to be gained by thus joining what should be separated, and separating what should be joined."

One of his first examples of objects of definition is the exact meaning, debated over and over again, of the term *clan*. This is a matter that he was to take up again ten years later in *The Progress of Man.*[17] Endless definitions of the clan have been proposed, he writes, but these have been vitiated by a technical distinction, taken to be fundamental, between patrilineal and matrilineal descent. This, however, is to overlook the fact that "classifications based on a single character are as valueless in the science of culture as in biology: they must be based on the whole structure." It so happens, Hocart states, that this particular character is of secondary importance, and, "in fact, the distinction between patrilineal and matrilineal is far from absolute." All the same, a concern to define the clan (or lineal descent group) has continued to occupy social anthropologists, and even in modern discussions the presumption lingers that patriliny and matriliny, though not sufficient to establish the type of a society, are in themselves principles of organization.[18] Only more recently has it been proposed that an empirical definition of descent groups as "patrilineal," "matrilineal," etc., should be given up altogether.[19] This recommendation, it may be suggested, is a fitting culmination to Hocart's reiterated criticism of the reliance upon definition. Although it is the conclusion to a formal argument, in contrast to Hocart's historical intention, the method is nevertheless apt to the task of an evolutionary reconstruction of changing systems. The study of structural change, by reference to logical possibilities and to formal constraints on the evolution of historical societies, can provide a clear test case of the process of convergence that Hocart delineates. The terminologies of societies of very different forms, prescriptive and nonprescriptive, can in the course of varied influences by disparate factors, and after undergoing their several trains of individual changes, come to resemble one another remarkably closely, i.e., to converge in common into a distinct type of social classification.[20]

As Hocart writes at the conclusion of the essay, "Convergence undoubtedly exists and common origins undoubtedly exist. The structure of all institutions, when sufficiently known, will point with no uncertain finger one way or the other." In the recent analyses just alluded to, however, the indications are supplied not merely by a sufficiency of knowledge, but by a revived application of Hocart's method: namely the abjuration of substantive definitions, the concentration on historical change, and the exercise of the widest comparison.

Chapter 3, "Psychology and Ethnology," takes up the comparably fundamental question about the connection between institutions and the states of mind of those who live by them.

This is a long-standing problem, and in attempts to answer it the usual temptation has been to infer the one type of phenomenon from the other. Hocart sets out to demonstrate that "the mental operations of a people cannot be deduced from the customs they practice, or their customs deduced from their mental operations." Viewed against the prior history of sociological thought, this contention might be taken simply as a confirmation of Durkheim's arguments about the autonomy of social facts and the fallaciousness of trying to explain them directly by individual psychology.[21] Hocart's essay, however, has the distinct value and advantage that it is not merely deductive, but derives from the immediacy of living among Fijians and from seeing while with them whether their motives could be matched to their conduct, as Frazer and others of the day had contended. Hence, in particular, his ability to turn the psychological hypothesis so ironically back on its proponents with the report that: "It is because savages interpret our customs psychologically that they think us wicked, or daft, or both." Moreover, as he goes on to show, we are ignorant even of the true motives and emotions of our contemporaries and countrymen, so that the approach fails to work in the best of cases, let alone in conjecturing the origins of institutions or the purposes of those who maintain them. And, in any case, we can do without such psychological fictions, just as we manage quite well in the study of architecture or kinship.

Arguments so clear and cogent as these were remarkable enough when first published in 1915, but what is perhaps yet more remarkable is that the very type of psychological explanation that Hocart inveighed against can still be revived in modern social anthropology,[22] and that an attempt to refute the explanation of institutions by reference to individual sentiments can stir some controversy.[23] It is something of a question, however, whether even a direct analytical confrontation can prove decisive in shaping professional opinion. If neither Durkheim nor Hocart was successful it may be that no such general revision of outlook is to be looked for. Given the intentionality of much human behavior, together with the psychoanalytical tendencies in European mental therapy, historiography, and fiction, it is perhaps to be expected, rather, that a dominant recourse in the interpretation of social life will continue to be psychological. For that matter, there is no reason in principle that it should not be so; it is, indeed, a type of explanation that on occasion may well be right, in part, or at least help toward the better recognition of the complex grounds of social forms. But this very promise makes it the more advisable to bear in mind Hocart's conclusion that "a customary action is no clue to the state of mind behind it,"[24] and to reassess against his arguments the attractive plausibility of a purely psychological explanation.

A main lesson urged by Hocart's essay, definite though its contentions are, is not to be doctrinaire on such matters but to make a more balanced and practical estimation of the explanatory alternatives that are appropriate to each case. As in Hocart's writings in general, the clarity of expression and the firmness of his conclusions should not be taken for dogma. He did not intend them as such, and to construe them so rigidly would be quite false to the style of thought he exemplifies and which should be the first profit in returning to his writings.

In "Myths in the Making" (Chapter 4) Hocart advances from his argument, in "The Common Sense of Myth,"[25] that a myth can be explained by making a systematic cultural study of the region in which it is found.

This is, of course, too unqualified a precept to serve for general application, and Hocart resumes his characteristic approach when, by making a systematic comparison, he proposes a common origin of Vedic and Fijian ritual; yet the emphasis on common sense is maintained in his contention that the gods of the forefathers of those cultures, incarnate in kings and priests, actually did what the texts and traditions say they did. In a field of study so open to fantasy and sophistry, the argument of this essay makes the sober injunction that we begin a consideration of myth by taking it as it stands. To do so may not lead us very far, but it makes an eminently sensible start—and "why choose the more difficult explanation, when there is an easier one to hand?"

Not that Hocart is simplistic or deliberately conservative in his approach; on the contrary, he considerably anticipates at one point the procedure elaborated far more recently by a most sophisticated student of myth: Lévi-Strauss, in presenting a structural analysis of myth, makes it a point of method to define a given myth as consisting of all of its versions. Thus Freud's interpretation of the Oedipus tale has to be included among the recorded versions compared, and a structural analysis should take the modern construct into account just as much as the drama of Sophocles.[26] It is an interesting detail in the history of ideas that Hocart, in 1922, had already treated the modern gloss of a classical scholar as "a continuation of myth building." This, he observed, may seem strange, for we are accustomed to assume that "the creation of myths involves mental processes that have nothing in common with the inferences of a scholar"; but if we decline to admit a psychological difference, then the consequence follows that both myth and commentary should be treated together.

With Chapter 5, on the early Indo-European kinship system, we come to a topic of great historical importance. This essay, perhaps because of its place of publication, has since been largely overlooked, but it is a piece of work in which, in 1928, Hocart made a serious contribution that abundantly deserves a sustained notice.

In 1889 Delbrück had published an authoritative study of "Indo-Germanic" kinship terms,[27] but, as Hocart begins by saying, he did not definitely state what kind of system the early Indo-Europeans possessed, nor did he consider the possible connections with "the cross-cousin system." Hocart's aim, working from the basis of Delbrück's materials[28] and supplementing these mainly with data from India and Ceylon, was to answer these questions, and his analyses marked a definite advance in the reconstruction of the archaic forms of Indo-European society. His conclusions were that the Indo-European system was at one time classificatory, but that it was not of what he called "the cross-cousin type." By this latter designation he referred to a terminology expressing a constant marriage with the bilateral cross-cousin; i.e., in a more recent description, a two-line terminology of prescriptive alliance.

Three points in his argument have a special technical interest. First, he remarks that the words for "in-laws" are remarkably constant in Indo-European languages, and "this alone is sufficient evidence that the original system was not a cross-cousin one." In other words, and conversely, Hocart recognizes what we today would call a prescriptive terminology[29] partly by its lack of separate terms for affines. In doing so, he anticipates by some years Lowie's more explicit and prominent observation that "a feature worth noting [in Australian terminologies] is the absence of terms of affinity. This is evidently to be correlated with the fact that in Australia marriage is prescribed with definite blood relatives. Accordingly there is no necessity for coining new words for connections by marriage."[30] It is only far more recently that this has become recognized as a regular and distinctive feature of prescriptive terminologies,[31] and Hocart deserves belated credit for having made the point at so early a stage in such inquiries.

The second technical point is Hocart's suggestion that "special terms for grandparents seem to form an organic part of a cross-cousin system."

> In fact, a perfect cross-cousin system seems to involve different terms for the father's father and the mother's father, since they belong to different groups, one being a straight relation, the other a crossed one; and the same applies to grandmother.

Empirically, this is not quite so, as Hocart certainly knew from his own work on Fiji: many two-line terminologies do not make such distinctions,[32] and Dumont has even presented an argument intended to show why, in a South Indian terminology of the kind, the two grandfathers "cannot be distinguished."[33] Nevertheless, Hocart's observation was a logical one, simply extrapolating to the limit the systematic principles that order the medial levels, and it directed attention to what was to be taken up as an interesting diagnostic feature in the study of prescriptive forms of social classification.

Finally, the third technical point to be mentioned is Hocart's concentration on the "confusion of grandfather and uncle, grandson and nephew." He compares this Indo-European feature with the custom in Vanua Levu, Fiji, of identifying the mother's father and the mother's brother, so that "the mother's brother is called grandfather, and the sister's son grandson." But he immediately remarks that this seems to be correlated with the custom by which a man calls his father's sister "elder sister," and, as he points out, of this custom there is no trace in Indo-European languages. His approach is thus systematic and comparative, so that in order to estimate the possible significance of one terminological equation he at once looks for its formal correlates in the reciprocal statuses of the classification, and to grasp the principle he looks for parallel usages in different and contemporary societies. That this is not an inevitable or obvious recourse, especially in 1928, might readily be shown by contrast with more recent analyses which entail correlates not testified to by Indo-European vocabularies, and which reconstruct the original system without considering the actual incidence in known societies of the features postulated.

In his conclusions, Hocart is definite that the archaic Indo-European system was not based on bilateral cross-cousin marriage (symmetric alliance), but he nevertheless glimpses certain hints of this type of organization in a number of isolated and otherwise unresolved problems, in particular the indication of a special connection between grandfather and grandson. This last feature has not, in fact, as we can now more confidently state, the diagnostic value that Hocart attributes to it, but there is no denying that in estimating the character and extension of the Indo-European system it is essential to take into account the prescriptive systems of India and Ceylon. As Hocart ends, anyone who can decide the question will have written "a most important chapter in the history of the development of European society."

To the present, however, neither the original nature of Indo-European terminologies nor their relation to prescriptive systems has been satisfactorily worked out. Friedrich, in an admirable linguistic conspectus of these matters,[34] largely confirms the classical findings of Delbrück, Schrader, and other predecessors, but in his sociological suggestions he unfortunately is led astray by his anthropological authorities. The PIE terminology, he concludes, was in part ordered in accordance with something called the "Omaha III skewing rule," and he further writes that the PIE features in question are "diagnostic of Omaha systems found in many parts of the world."[35] But the analytical apparatus on which he is led to rely rests on very uncertain grounds: a gratuitously intricate technique, derived from mere assumptions of a highly disputable kind, produces no more than a narrow and inconsequential typology, and the stock "Omaha" type, as thus elaborated, is rendered an even more misleading reification. The PIE terminology does indeed contain some interesting, if rather sporadic, evidences of lineal or quasi-lineal identifications and their correlates, but nothing at all has been understood or otherwise achieved by characterizing PIE society as "a system of the Omaha type."[36] On the question of cross-cousin marriage, too, Friedrich is misled, only this time in part by his reliance on the authority of Hocart himself. He correctly accepts Hocart's argument that the terms for affines argue against a prescriptive system, but he has not the evidence he supposes when he also cites Hocart in his conclusion that "the absence of specific terms for the grandparents [argues] strongly against a cross-cousin system."[37]

The problem of descent and marriage in early Indo-European society has more recently received its most substantial modern treatment at the masterly hands of Emile Benveniste,[38] and with these new scholarly considerations on the part of so eminent a scholar the issues are at last adequately exposed for renewed analysis, both formal and sociological.[39] However, Benveniste's own reconstruction of the marriage system, with particular reference to the so-called "Omaha" feature (Lat. *avus-avunculus*), can hardly be accepted in the light of modern studies of terminology and alliance.[40] Even his authoritative linguistic investigations serve, in the end, simply to emphasize that the real nature of proto-Indo-European kinship has yet to be ascertained. In this revived enterprise Hocart's essay acquires a new importance.

The essay on "Buddha and Devadatta" (Chapter 6) makes a more particular continuation of the theme of Indo-European kinship and cross-cousin marriage.

Hocart offers the interesting suggestion that the apparent enmity between Buddha and his cousin Devadatta is an echo of the friendly and ceremonial antagonism of cross-cousins associated with bilateral cross-cousin marriage in Fiji. The inference is supported by comparison with Ceylon and South India, in areas characterized by the same form of alliance, and Hocart ultimately conjectures a more general source of social antagonisms in the rivalry between two intermarrying groups.

In this essay are expressed two of Hocart's didactic preoccupations: the historical unity of systems of bilateral cross-cousin marriage, wherever they may be found around the world,[41] and the "theology" of which the intermarriage is only one aspect. These are large matters involving, in any scholarly assessment, the comparative analysis of systems of prescriptive alliance, the "total" character of such systems as symbolic forms, the relation of opposition,[42] the explanation of joking relationships, and much else. To adduce the lessons of modern investigations into all of these issues would make too lengthy a commentary on the particular problem considered in the essay, but one can again stress, Hocart's role in 1923 (when the article was first published) as a pioneer in theoretical undertakings that have since become exceedingly prominent in social anthropology.[43]

On a point of method, also, the essay shows Hocart's typical procedure: he takes an apparently isolated tradition, then seeks structural parallels in other societies, and concludes by referring the institution to a more fundamental metaphysics. It is this quest for the most distant historical connections, and the ultimate ideological implications, that many find so exciting an aspect of anthropology and that Hocart so well puts into effect.

Chapter 8, "Many-armed Gods," introduces yet another aspect of Hocart's eclectic interests.

Macdonell had published a paper on "The Development of Early Hindu Iconography"[44] in which he examined what he regarded as the "monstrosity" of representing gods with more than the natural number of arms. Since the volume in which it appeared had a limited circulation, at the beginning of World War I, Macdonell published the gist of his article under the same title in an orientalist journal,[45] and it was this that Hocart commented on.

The conclusions of Macdonell's argument were that many-armed images were an historical development, and that "the purpose of the innovation was the practical one of supplying a means of displaying the symbols without which the gods could not be adequately identified when represented by themselves apart from the adjunct of a *vāhana* [vehicle]." That is, the gods' natural pairs of arms were already engaged in blessing or teaching or whatever they were expressing, and so they could not hold the attributes (such as axe, noose, conch, trident, and so on) which traditionally characterized their activities and by which their images were to be identified. It was for this reason, Macdonell proposed, that the extra arms were added.

Hocart's response to this argument is characteristically straightforward and cogent: the attributes can be represented without sticking on extra arms; some statues have several heads, so that the many arms are part of a more general artistic development; other statues have more than two pairs of arms, though none of them holds any attribute; the presence or absence of additional arms follows definite conventions, so that one and the same god may be represented with two or with more arms according to the aspect or personage portrayed.

The outcome is that the origin of many-armed gods was not occasioned by the practical difficulty of providing enough hands to put the attributes in, but that "theological considerations were paramount in deciding the number of arms." Equally typically, moreover, Hocart does not confine himself to statuary alone, not even in the wider sphere of Greece and Egypt to which he extends his comparison, but draws an unexpected parallel with the development of musical taste. He ends his paper with a query that even more has his own ring: "The main problem, however, is not so much how the conception got into art, as how it got into the human mind."

Although it is perhaps Hocart's style of thought that will evoke the wider interest in this essay, it has been found a cogent contribution to Hindu iconography. Banerjea finds Macdonell's argument difficult to accept, and, quoting Hocart on the paramountcy of theological considerations, supports instead the view that the many hands and their attributes portray attempts to symbolize the multifarious activities of the gods.[46]

The concluding essay, on "Rotation" (Chapter 9), laconic though it is, makes a fitting termination to this volume, for it gives a lapidary expression to Hocart's usual progress of ideas.

He starts from Horwitz's articles on the evolution of the wheel and other rotating machines, and at once he goes to the central issue, which is not a mechanical device but a principle: "We shall never get far if we are content to study the potter's wheel only, or the chariot wheel only, or the spindle only; we must take rotation as the object of our study and take into account all the contrivances in which it may be exemplified." But even technically there is a problem that has been neglected by technologists because of their prejudicial separation of things and ideas. Rotation on fixed bearings produces friction, and friction reduces momentum and hence the usefulness of the device. Lubrication is the answer to this, but where does the idea of lubrication come from? Not necessarily or simply from difficulties encountered in mechanics. Ritual anointing with oil, or rubbing with fat, is much more ancient, Hocart claims, than the lubrication of machines. Men who had no notion of reducing mechanical friction, therefore, were well acquainted with the slippery properties of oil and fat. Hence, the experience gained in anointing an image or a candidate could have contributed to the technical discovery.

In another of his works, however, Hocart had already acknowledged that this ritual knowledge by no means leads inevitably to the technical application. Men who oil their bodies readily become aware of the lubricity of oil, yet they may never think of applying it to mechanical work. "I cannot think of a single use of lubricants by Fijians in mechanics; yet they give their pregnant women 'a slippery medicine' to make it easy . . . for the child to be born."[47] The point, therefore, is not to claim a fixed order in discoveries, but to argue that mechanical procedures do not always originate in mechanics.

Beneath this persuasive argument, of course, runs Hocart's deeper preoccupation with ritual and with the ideas and values that inspire symbolism as the primal expression of many human concerns that only later assume such apparently disparate institutionalized forms as kingship, government, or intermarriage. Basic to these theoretical interests is the attitude declared in Hocart's concluding line: "Man's mind is not thus divided into watertight compartments."

The editing of this collection has consisted mainly in the selection and arrangement of the essays. These have been ordered not chronologically but by theme and character, the wider and more abstract topics being placed first, then the Indo-European and Indian investigations, and finally the note that looks technological in subject but which turns out to direct attention back to far larger issues.

A few of the bibliographical references have been amplified or supplied, but since the original citations provide adequate indication of Hocart's sources it has not been thought necessary to extend each one with complete particulars. At a number of places the punctuation has tacitly been made clearer, and British spellings have been exchanged for American. The diagrams for Chapter 5, which were defective, have been improved. A general index has been added, and the whole has undergone light copy editing.

The frontispiece plate is reproduced from a portrait sketch painted in Cairo by N. Labouchère in 1939, the year of Hocart's death. The original belonged to his widow, the late Mrs. E. G. Hocart, who bequeathed it to the Royal Anthropological Institute.

RODNEY NEEDHAM
All Souls College, Oxford

1

Evidence in Human History

Progress in the understanding of man's evolution, especially his mental evolution, is being hampered by popular fallacies concerning evidence. The nature of evidence is the same in all walks of life. It is the same in the courts of law as it is in science; only in the courts the rules of evidence are not usually distorted by prejudice and fanaticism, as they constantly are in science, especially the science of man, which so often skirts the passions of politics and religion. We cannot do better, then, than begin our study of evidence in the courts.

They distinguish two kinds of evidence: the direct and the circumstantial. If a witness actually saw the murder and describes it, it is direct evidence. But it is rare that a murder is actually witnessed. It is then necessary to note every circumstance: the state and position of the victim, clues as to time, the movements of the victim and of the suspect, their conditions and characters, to interpret all these data in accordance with the laws of nature, especially human nature, and to frame a theory which explains them all, and to which there is no imaginable alternative. That is circumstantial evidence.

There is a popular, but natural, delusion that direct evidence is neces-

Psyche Annual, vol. 13, 1933, pp. 80–93. Reprinted, with alterations, as Chap. 1 in Hocart, *Kings and Councillors* (Cairo 1936; second impression, edited and with an introduction by Rodney Needham, Chicago: University of Chicago Press, 1970).

sarily better than circumstantial, in fact that it is the only satisfactory kind of evidence. A learned judge in summing up a famous murder trial rebutted this opinion. He pointed out that direct evidence might be the weaker of the two: the witness might be lying or biassed, his memory might be at fault, or his imagination be playing tricks. Even two witnesses might mislead. There are countries where fifty eyewitnesses all telling the same story could not be trusted. On the other hand, when a hundred little details which no man could have premeditated or arranged all point in one direction, and one direction only, the certainty is as great as is ever to be attained in human affairs. Probably no man has ever been hanged in the last hundred years on direct evidence unsupported by circumstantial. Many have been hanged on circumstantial evidence alone.

The historian as a rule shares the popular prejudice: he pins his faith to direct evidence, to the writings of contemporaries, to coins, to ruins. Circumstantial evidence he distrusts and even fears. He clings to his direct evidence as a timid sailor to the coast. If anyone proposes to strike across the sea with the guidance of compass alone he makes a virtue of his timidity, and converts it into a lofty superiority.

Even the physical anthropologist has been inclined of late to trust to the direct evidence of fossils to the exclusion of the circumstantial evidence yielded by living specimens. Yet he ought to know better, for he has approached the study of human evolution, not from the side of history, which has long been enslaved by its fossils, antiquities, but from the side of science, which has long been familiar with circumstantial evidence. When a scientist sets up a working hypothesis he is doing under a grander name what the detective does who has no direct evidence.

Physical anthropologists might remember that Laplace outlined the history, not of man, but of the whole solar system, a history reckoned not in thousands, but in millions of years, outlined it without any records, simply from circumstantial evidence. He noted the nebulae, he noted the suns, he noted the dead stars; these and many other things he supposed represented different stages through which our own solar system had passed. He found that he could in this way explain the present behavior of the sun and its planets. The main lines of his nebular hypothesis still hold. It has been emended because it did not explain all the circumstances, not because there was no direct evidence. The details may have been questioned, but never the method. Both he and his revisers worked by the comparative method, though they may not have called it so. They compared the varieties of stellar systems, and tried to imagine some form from which they could be derived.

Biology itself has achieved its most notable successes purely by the use of circumstantial evidence. A biologist has recently declared: "Evolution itself is accepted by zoologists, *not because it has been observed to occur* or is supported by logically coherent arguments, but *because it does fit all the facts* of Taxonomy, of Palaeontology, and of Geographical Distribution, and *because no alternative explanation is credible.*" Biology, unlike astronomy, has something like direct evidence in the shape of bones and imprints of extinct animals. This evidence is called paleontology; but it is both inadequate and superfluous for the theory of evolution; it has supplied welcome confirmation or amendments, has filled in details, but was never indispensable to the main theory. The theory of evolution was not based on paleontology, but rather it was the other way round. Evolution provided a new use for fossils. It set men looking for them with greater zeal, because it gave them a worthier end than the mere collecting of specimens.

In no branch of biology has this been so much the case as in human biology. It had no paleontology before Darwin. Or rather it did not realize it had. The first Gibraltar skull was discovered in 1848: it passed quite unnoticed. *The Origin of Species* appeared in 1859. It was not till men had become thoroughly used to the idea of man's descent from an ape-like creature that the skull was brought out of its obscurity, having ceased to be a curio and become a link in the evidence. It was not the direct evidence of a missing link that converted biologists. Rather, having been converted by comparative evidence, they set out to find direct evidence in the shape of fossil men in order to confirm their deductions and complete the confusion of their opponents. It took thirty-five years of *The Origin of Species* to set them really looking. Then Dubois went out to find the ape-like fossil and found it. Since then discovery has succeeded discovery, and the illusion of direct evidence has taken possession of the minds of anthropologists. One leading authority tells us that "for the *serious* study of race history those characters are of special value which can be distinguished in the skeleton, as we naturally know nothing about the skin and hair characters for prehistoric man save by the *risky* analogy from modern men." He forgets that it was on the "risky analogy" of modern species that Darwin and Wallace based their theory of evolution. They risked and they won; for in science, too, faint heart never won fair lady.

I say the "illusion of direct evidence" because when we examine this direct evidence we find it is not direct after all. Not one of the skulls older than the Upper Paleolithic represents an ancestor of ours. The anthropologist cannot say, "This skull represents our ancestors as they were 200,000 years ago, and this is exactly how they looked." He can only say, "Here is a skull of an animal so like man that I must *suppose* him to be descended from the ape-like man which Darwin postulated. I suppose it because I have been converted to evolution by Darwin's arguments. I think it is the only theory that will account for all the facts, including the facts of this skull. By making this supposition I invest this skull with a new interest: it is no longer an isolated fact; it is another pointer in my search for circumstantial evidence. That pointer helps to narrow the field within which I must look for the characteristics of the hypothetical ancestor; it defines them more narrowly." All these skulls are in the end so much more fuel for the comparative method. That is why they probably never have converted a single opponent of evolution. He who is not already a convert will never be converted by Pithecanthropus or by Piltdown Man. Rather, the voluminous controversy that has grown up round these meager and uncertain remains has been eagerly seized upon by the fundamentalists to discredit the whole theory of evolution.

The craze for direct evidence has prevented a comparative psychology from developing. A beginning was made towards 1900. It was known, for instance, that individuals vary considerably in their color vision; that some cannot distinguish certain shades of green from certain shades of red. It occurred to the Cambridge Expedition to the Torres Straits to institute a comparison between races in this respect. Rivers found only one doubtful case of color blindness out of 152, but later he found that 12·8 male Todas in every hundred are color blind. A comparative survey of the world might enable us to draw inferences as to the color vision of primitive man. The method could be extended to other mental characteristics of modern races, but there are no fossil sensations or emotions that we can touch and see, and so an age which confuses reality with visibility and touchability, which thinks a thing real in proportion as it is hard, will have nothing to do with a comparative study of the human mind. The mirage of direct evidence has lured the students of human evolution from one half of the human being, leaving the physical side unintelligible, for you cannot separate physical and mental.

It is in the evolution of culture that the cult of direct evidence has been carried furthest. That kind of evidence is, or rather seems, so abundant that there is no need for any other. There are manuscripts, inscriptions, pots, and buildings galore; so the popular belief in the infallibility of direct evidence can be indulged to the full. This naive faith in the evidence of our eyes is all the more remarkable as the nineteenth century and the first quarter of the twentieth have been largely spent by historians in discrediting that very kind of evidence on which they rely. Niebuhr led with an attack on the early Roman tradition, which had been accepted without question. But the critics were not long content with demolishing legends; they soon were emboldened to attack the great names among historians. Thucydides was a contemporary of the events he recorded and an actor in some. His testimony had never been doubted. Yet the liberal Grote convicted him of being a biased Tory traducing the Greek democrats. Herodotus may be credulous, but his honesty has never been questioned. He based his narrative of the Persian Wars on the evidence of eyewitnesses; but scholars infected by the fashionable skepticism went to Marathon to see for themselves, and proved on the ground that his account of the battle was impossible, and some even proved to their satisfaction that the Persians, not the Greeks, had won the battle. Moral judgments have been reversed wholesale, heroes have been deposed, and Neroes have been held up as model emperors. One wonders that after this orgy of skepticism any one should go on writing history at all. Many historians have thought to find more solid foundations in the hard material turned up by the spade. Inscriptions have been collected as a check on writers, but inscriptions are no more trustworthy than writings. They seldom are candid, and often are inscribed by way of flattery or propaganda. They may record the sort of thing a great king would do rather than what he actually did, and they are silent about his failures. In any case they usually refer to events which seemed most important at the time, but which do not help us in the least to understand the evolution of culture. Pots and pans do not lie; but that is because they do not speak. Their chief use, apart from throwing some light on crafts, is to give us dates; but what is the use of dates without facts to fit into them?

No wonder that in despair many have turned away from history as a game of pure conjecture. They feel like a judge in an Oriental court after hearing fifty lying witnesses, and hopeless of ever fixing the right and the wrong of the case because his detectives have supplied him with no circumstantial evidence with which to check the statements. Those who still retain an interest in the history of man see no hope of ever tracing the evolution of his ideas, except in so far as they may be stamped on hard, imperishable things like bones or stones. They assure us that we shall never know the beliefs of Neolithic Man, because beliefs do not get petrified. We can touch skeletons and so we may get some idea what their notions of death may have been; but how can we ever know what their social organization was like, or their marriage and birth rites, which do not get solidified, and so yield no direct evidence?

The fact is when they say we can never know, what they really mean is they cannot see the way by which we can know, so they do not think any one else can, which is rather an arrogant assumption. They should remember that Auguste Comte once cited as an example of knowledge to which we could never attain the chemical composition of stars. A few years later Kirchoff applied spectral analysis to the stars, and provided that very information which Comte had just declared to be unknowable. The fact is men do not begin to proclaim a discovery impossible until they begin to contemplate its possibility. It is an augury that the discovery is at hand.

There is one branch of human history which, like the biology of protozoa, has no direct evidence to build on, and no hope of any. That is comparative philology. No one expects that we shall ever recover documents containing specimens of that lost speech from which Latin, Greek, Sanskrit, English, and such languages are descended. Writing was not adopted by its users till long after it had split up into languages very distinct from one another. Our earliest Greek inscriptions go back only to the sixth century B.C., at the very least a millenium and a half after this splitting up. The absence of all direct evidence and of all hope of acquiring it has proved a blessing in disguise. It has forced linguists to do without it, to drop the wasteful and ineffective frontal attack to which archaeologists are addicted, for a more decisive and economical flanking movement. They have been driven to the comparative method.

That method is based on the existence of divergence: if a species has diverged in different directions, giving rise to a variety of new species, it must be possible to trace back their lines of divergence till they converge on one point, the hypothetical extinct ancestor. Every offspring reproduces its parent or imitates it, but with a difference, which is not the same in all the offspring. By comparing all the descendants or derivatives we can eliminate all the differences, leaving only what they have in common, and that is presumably what they hold from the lost original. We can never draw conclusions as to that original from one derivative only. If we confined our attention to the Northern Europeans only we could only imagine that primitive man was fair-skinned. Other races, however, have other colors, so we must attribute to primitive man some color from which all the existing ones can be derived. If we only knew English we should believe that a man had never called the woman who bore him anything else but "mother." Other languages, however, call her *mutter, matar, meter,* and so on. We must derive all these variants from some form which accounts for them all.

The test of these assumptions lies in their results. While the believers in the direct method still dispute who were the Greeks, whether Zeus was once a powerful king or a natural phenomenon, where the Neolithic Folk came from, or how the Piltdown skull ought to be restored, the conclusions of the comparative philologists are in the main so well established that the subject has fallen into stagnation because there is little to dispute about, and controversy is the life of science. No one now disputes that Latin, Greek, and the rest are branches of the same tree; no one questions the main characteristics of the parent tongue. A great many words have been identified in the derivative languages once for all. Thus there is no going back on such equivalences as English *father* = Latin *pater* = Greek *pater* = Sanskrit *pitar* = Old Irish *athir,* etc.

It is strange then that there is no more determined opponent of the extension of the comparative method to other branches of culture than the comparative philologist. He is positive it will not work in religion or social organization. Well, the best answer to that is not to argue about principles, not to insist that there is only one method in all science, but to get down to work, and to show by example that exactly the same procedure is applicable to theology and to social organization as to language, and produces results as certain as anything in science.

Let anyone take up a dictionary of classical antiquities or mythology and look up what the believers in direct evidence have done with Hermes. However devoted they may be to the records which they can handle and read with their eyes, they cannot be content with the bare facts (no intelligent being can be); they must try and explain them. Scholars and antiquarians have variously explained Hermes as darkness, dawn, twilight, the wind, a god of the infernal regions, a solar god. All these suggestions, unfortunately, are incapable of proof because the true nature of Hermes was forgotten, it is evident, long before our records begin. We could go on piling texts upon texts and get no further in certainty, since we should be getting no further back in time. The suggestions remain suggestions. This battle of conjectures is characteristic of those who will admit nothing but direct evidence. They are like men trying to draw a line from a known point to an unknown one without any idea of the distance and very little of the direction. We must draw lines from at least two points to converge on the point we are seeking. Greece alone can never give us direction or distance. Let us take India as our second point.

We cannot read an account of the Vedic god Agni, that is Fire, without being struck by some resemblance to Hermes. Superficial resemblance, however, is not enough: it classes fishes with whales, swallows with swifts. As in zoology, so in cultural studies, we must penetrate below the surface and dissect the structure. Let us dissect Agni and Hermes in parallel columns.[1]

AGNI	HERMES
1. Is fire, and is born of the fire sticks.	1. Inventor of fire and the fire sticks (H.H. IV, 111).
2. Is more particularly the sacrificial fire.	2. —
3. As such he conducted the first sacrifice (Rgv. III, 15, 14; V. 3, 5).	3. After inventing fire he holds a burnt sacrifice, necessarily the first (H.H. IV, 115).
4. As such he both conveys the offerings to the gods, and partakes himself.	4. He "lusts after the rite of eating the sacrificial meat," but refrains and holds a sacrifice for twelve gods, of whom he apparently is one.
5. As such he is the intermediary between gods and men, their messenger.	5. Messenger of the gods. Intermediary between gods and men.
6. With the offerings he conveys the sacrificer (spiritually) to the gods; makes him one with the gods.	6. Conveys heroes to heaven on apotheosis, e.g., Herakles, Dionysos.

7. Is also the altar on which the fire is made.	7. —
8. Is also the cremation fire.	8. —
9. As such conveys the dead to the underworld.	9. Conveys souls to Hades, and so is called 'Escort of Souls.'
10. Priest and chaplain of the gods.	10. Herald of the gods.
11. Is threefold, that is has three aspects.	11. Called 'Thrice-great' (late), 'Three-headed.'
12. One form of Agni is called 'The Face.'	12. There is a Hermes Fore-fighter, and one Army-leader.
13. As Face of the Army, that is as leader, the general sacrifices to Agni, the Face.	13. The Attic generals sacrificed to Hermes Hegemonios, Leader of the Army.
14. Abounds in semen (*Rgv.* IV, 5, 2).	14. Has images with erect phallus (Herodotos, II, 51).
15. Associated with the ram.	15. Associated with the he-goat and the ram.
16. Agni is cattle and bestower of cattle (*S.B.*, VI, 3, 1, 32; *Rgv.*, I, 127, 10).	16. Receives from Apollo the rule over cattle and all four-footed beasts. He is called "cattle-driving", 'sheep-tending' (*H.H.*, IV, 134; 491 ff.; 567 ff.).
17. Bestows wealth.	17. Called 'Giver of good things'.
18. —	18. Protector of traders and travellers (*Hodios*).
19. Called 'slayer of demons,' (Rgv. X, 87, 1), also 'Slayer of Vritra.'	19. Called 'Slayer of Argus'.
20. —	20. Invents the lyre and the panpipe.
21. Identified with the sun.	21. Some scholars have taken him for a sun god.
22. Kindled at dawn (*S.B.* II, 3, 1, 15), and so is called 'waking at dawn' (*usarbudh*).	22. Some have thought him to be dawn.
23. Kindled three times a day.	23. Born in the morning he develops in three stages in one day.
24.	24. Called 'leader of dreams.'
25. —	25. Chief of thieves.

Therefore Agni = Hermes.

They agree so closely, even to small details, that we cannot resist this conclusion: it is not a resemblance of appearance but of structure. There is, however, on the right-hand side an important blank: there is nothing to indicate what was the nature of Hermes. He invented fire, but is nowhere identified with fire. The word Agni, on the other hand, means fire, and his nature is clearly defined over and over again in the texts. We are faced with two alternatives: one is that the parent conception was that of a fire-god; the other is that it was not, and the idea of fire was added in the Indian branch after it had begun to diverge from the Greek, that it was a reinterpretation of an original god who was not fire. We have no direct evidence to decide between those alternatives. There is no test but the usual one in circumstantial evidence: which assumption explains the facts? The second one explains nothing, but leaves us with a host of difficulties. The first one explains satisfactorily most of the characteristics of Hermes. It explains why he is an intermediary between men and gods, for the sacrificial fire conveys the offerings; why he conveys men to the gods, for the sacrifice brings the sacrificer into communion with the gods; why he guides the souls to the nether regions, because fire takes the deceased thither. To be the intermediary between gods and men is the same as being the priest or the herald. The sacred fire in India was carried before a migrating tribe, in Sparta before an army on the warpath. Hence Agni is the Face of the Army, Hermes the Fore-fighter. The association with cattle is more obscure, but cattle are the most important sacrificial victim; the sacrificial fire feeds largely on its flesh. The sun is fire, it is Agni in heaven, so it is not surprising that Hermes should have been taken for a sun-god.

The argument is exactly the same as that which decides whether the lizard is more primitive in retaining four legs, or the glass snake in never having grown any. The first alternative commends itself because it explains the presence of rudimentary legs underneath the skin of the blind worm; the second explains nothing. Paleontology, by supplying direct evidence of the succession of types, may confirm the deductions of the zoologist and fill in the details, but it is not necessary to the main conclusion.

A comparison of Agni and Hermes takes us no further back than the nearest common ancestor of both, which is only two or three thousand, perhaps four thousand, years B.C. We can work our way further back by enlarging our field, by calling in cultures that may have diverged at an earlier period still, such as the Sumerian. We can bring in living cultures in remote areas, which may also be earlier divergences. The Koryaks of Kamchatka recognize their fire-board, from which they make fire, as a god. He is an intermediary between gods and men, also god of the Koryak cattle, which consists of reindeer. The affinity is obvious, but our information is not full enough to decide whether the Koryak form diverged earlier or later than the Greek.

We can enlarge our inquiry in other ways than in space. We can regard Agni and Hermes as just items in each of two systems, Indian and Greek culture, like a tooth or an eye in two species of the same animal genus. They are homologies in two allied cultures.

We concluded that

Agni = Hermes.

We noted that

Agni = priest, Brahman;

and that

Hermes = herald, Kerux.

We can deduce that

Brahman = Kerux.

This homology has then to be put to the test by analyzing the nature and functions of the Indian Brahman and the Greek herald, even as we analyzed their gods. I will not carry out this analysis here, because this is not a treatise on the comparative study of Greek and Indian culture, but on the principles of evidence. I will, therefore, content myself with mentioning the fact that this analysis does work out and confirm the deduction.

It may be that some time the comparative history of culture will proceed by a series of deduction as in Euclid or a textbook of physics, in this form:

X is composed of A, B, C, D, R;
Y   "   "   A, B, C, D, S;
∴ X = Y and R = S.
And so on.

A treatise cast in that form would never be read as things are now. Physicists expect a chain of demonstrations. Historians are used to a discursive style, and will not read anything that is not literature. We must, therefore, as yet compromise and cast our argument into a fairly readable form without sacrificing too much of its rigor.

The comparative method in our example of Agni and Hermes reaches its goal more swiftly and certainly than the mere examination of records. It will be found to be so in every case. Scholars, historians, archaeologists, all the believers in direct evidence as the only one admissible, are wont to pile Pelion on Ossa without ever reaching higher than pure conjecture. They never reach in affairs two thousand years ago the certainty that evolution has attained to concerning developments that took place geological ages ago, and for which there is no direct evidence.

Another weakness of the direct method is that it fails to explain, and explanation is the end of science. The grammarian who sticks to his Greek texts, who will not adventure into what he regards as the quicksands of the comparative method, may note the facts of Greek Grammar; he cannot account for them. He cannot, for instance, tell you why Greek so often alternates *e* with *o*, as in legomen, legete; the comparative philologist can by calling Latin, Sanskrit, and the rest to his aid. He can postulate certain rules of the parent language that will account for all the facts of the derivative languages, and to which he can see no possible alternative.

Direct evidence not only fails to explain; it may even suggest the wrong explanation, not because it is in the least doubtful, but because it only tells us a fraction of the facts, while seeming to tell all. I have in mind a case from Fiji. I became acquainted there with a nobility, or royal family, if you like, which was divided into four clans, two of them alternating in the chieftainship, two of them out of the running. I was told exactly how it had been so divided, and why. It was not so very long ago that part of it, if not all, took place within the memory of the oldest men. The original family, descendants of a chief who lived just before 1800, had grown too large. As it was assessed at the same rate as the small clans, it was not bearing its fair share of the public contributions. Therefore the youngest branch, which we shall call D, was split off. Then as the remainder grew A was set apart. Of the remainder, B was zealous in public affairs, C neglected them for private work. In order to compel C to pull its own weight it was cut off from B. Had I confined my attention to this one village, as scholars confine themselves to Greece, or Rome, or Egypt, I might have rested content with this bit of local history, and taken this fourfold division to be a local accident. But the same arrangement of four clans, two qualified for chieftainship, two excluded, turned up in a neighboring tribe, then in another. It became quite impossible to accept the first case as the pure accident it seemed to be on the direct evidence, any more than we could accept as an accident the shape of a crystal repeated in experiment after experiment. The fourfold arrangement was a pattern into which Fijian royal families tended till recently to fall. The number four was doubtless connected with the ritual use of four, as in feasts, cures, etc. This fourfold division crops up again in Central Australia, in Java, in India, and is there connected with the four cardinal points of the compass. Evidently it is a very ancient pattern, since it is common to peoples so far removed from one another. It certainly never originated in Fiji. Yet the direct evidence supplied by the members of one family would lead one to think that it sprang up locally in the nineteenth century by the decision of one or two strong and able men. Are we to reject their evidence as lying? Certainly not: it tells us the truth, nothing but the truth, but not the whole truth. It tells us of certain passing maladjustments, such as are continually occurring in any community. It tells us how they were readjusted; it does not tell us of the immemorial tradition that there should be four clans, and that any readjustment should restore or retain that primeval arrangement. Nor does it tell us that there was not a fourfold arrangement before the readjustment.

To understand this let us suppose that Europe has been swept by a barbaric invasion that has destroyed all records, and even wiped out our social organization from the memory of men. America has escaped: it still has records of its constitution dating back to its original promulgation after the War of Independence. The historian would eagerly seize on these records, and would explain triumphantly to the learned world how parliamentary government originated. We know he would be quite wrong; that parliamentary government is vastly older than the eighteenth century; that in fact it never originated, but evolved insensibly out of some sort of assembly which it must be the task of historians of culture to define; that the American Constitution is merely a local modification of an ancient institution to meet local needs and satisfy philosophical theories which we can trace back through Rousseau, Locke, Hobbes, and right beyond them.

Again let us imagine that we have no records of any peerage before George I, that our earliest notice of any creation of peers is by that monarch. The historians would at once conclude that George I invented the peerage, and mistake his reasons for creating those particular peers for the motives that led to the institution of the peerage. It is as if a paleontologist were to say: "Here is a Pleistocene skull; it is the earliest that has ever been found. Here, then, we are assisting at the birth of mankind." That would be absurd; yet that is exactly what the historians continually are doing whenever they lose the scent in following it back; they commonly jump to the conclusion that the scent started there, not that it may have faded out. The Greeks are especially to blame for this bad habit. They tell us that Solon or Lykurgus promulgated such and such a law, state his reasons, and give us to understand that is how the law originated. Our historians too often are content and look no further. They forget that it is possible to promulgate an old law again, possibly with amendments. Parliament recently has voted against the Sunday opening of theatres, but that is not the origin of the custom. We know it can be traced back to the Hebrews. The recent Act merely reaffirms a modern application of a very ancient taboo. Absence of records means nothing: comparative evidence alone can decide. It so happens we have comparative evidence in the case of Lykurgus. We know that many of the institutions attributed to him existed in Crete. We can only conclude that they are much older than Lykurgus, that they go back at least as far as the nearest common ancestors of the Spartans and the Cretans. If these customs are included in the laws of Lykurgus it can only be that he reaffirmed or emended what he found already in existence. Tradition also says that Lykurgus imposed iron money on the Spartans, and gives his reason. But iron money is very widespread, and not peculiar to Sparta. Comparative evidence makes it impossible to believe that it originated in Sparta. If Lykurgus did include iron money in his constitution, he can have done no more than insist on its retention.

If the biologist wants to throw light on the origin of man he studies all the races at present in existence; he studies also the apes, the lemurs, and even the shrews. He tells the paleontologist what to look for, and the paleontologist looks for it. The historian of culture proceeds in exactly the opposite way. Ask him how the mendicant friars came into being, he will not cast round for living institutions so like the mendicant orders in structure as to be beyond doubt species of the same genus. No, he goes straight to his fossils, he ransacks libraries for documents, and in time produces a history, say, of the Grey Friars beginning with St. Francis. He tells you exactly on what occasion he instituted his order and what reasons he gave for doing so. He forgets to tell us what put these ideas into his head, whence came his inspiration; that he will never find in records. The authors of those records are not interested in anything but the personality of their hero, or they do not wish it to appear that St. Francis got his inspiration from anyone but God. Any suggestion that the model already existed, especially among the infidels, would be carefully suppressed. The records, then, can never explain why there is at that time an epidemic of mendicant orders: Crutched Friars ten years earlier in 1198 in Rome; Black Friars in 1215 in France; White Friars not till 1247, but originally appearing in the East in 1156. Remember, too, that any such widespread movement only succeeds after much pioneering: history only records the successes; it keeps no count of the preliminary failures. Who knows how many of these prepared the way for St. Francis, St. Dominic and the others? Evidently there was a wave; where did it start? Records cannot tell.

The comparative historian turns from them to living institutions. He finds in Ceylon one so similar that he must postulate a common origin. But who got it from whom? Here it is that direct evidence can come to the aid. Scholars and archaeologists can then bring their texts, their inscriptions, their bas-reliefs into play. They can trace the Sinhalese species back to Nepal in 500 B.C. They have direct evidence of its spread and of its westward missions as early as about 250 B.C. They can show that there was a considerable influx of Oriental ideas into Europe throughout the Middle Ages, that St. Josaphat is no other than the Buddha,[2] that the episode of the baskets in the Merry Wives of Windsor is depicted on an Indian bas-relief of the first century B.C., and generally reverse the idea that there was little or no communication between India and Western Europe in the Middle Ages. First, then, the comparative student can show that the Christian Friars are not an isolated phenomenon, but that begging monks are to be found also in Ceylon, Tibet, Japan. Then the student of records can supply documentary evidence that of these varieties the Sinhalese is the most primitive, that it best retains the characteristics of the parent form, which is attributed to the Buddha, but which was itself only one of many contemporary varieties, including one (Jainism) that still survives in India.

There are no records of the spread of mendicant orders from India to Europe. Neither is there any record that the anthropoid apes spread to Borneo and to Africa from a common center. We cannot *see* them spread and never shall. We may find a chain of fossil apes all the way from Malaysia to Central Africa, but that all these fossils have a common ancestor, and that this chain is due to spread, is pure assumption. It can never be proved if by proving we mean actually seeing it happen, or knowing someone who has seen it. But proof does not consist in seeing: it consists in providing so complete an explanation of the evidence of our senses that no better alternative can be thought of, an explanation which will enable us to move on to further conquests. In science, as in the courts, circumstantial evidence is not an inferior substitute for the evidence of eyes and ears: it is the very foundation of science, I should say of life. For we could never exist if we could not fill in the vast blanks in our perceptions with inference. Man was given a cerebral cortex to make good the deficiencies of his senses by combining their fragmentary messages into a body of knowledge on which he can act. Whether the historical sciences survive as such a body of knowledge, or perish as a mere mass of erudition, will depend on whether they have the courage to use the gift of nature or continue to believe only what they can see.

2

The Convergence of Customs

There has been much ado of late among anthropologists debating whether like customs must have a common origin or may be independent creations of minds working according to the same laws. There has been some feeling on both sides, one fails to see why; doubts never seem to have troubled the science of animals, which includes that of man, nor the science of language, which is included in it. Zoologists may have made mistakes in classing together animals that do not belong together; comparative philologists may be uncertain whether two words are the same or quite unconnected; but there seems to be no doubt about principles. It now has been recognized that the same conditions may mold different structures into the same forms, that environment may cause species wide apart to converge. On the other hand, this truth has not been used, or rather abused as it has been in the history of customs, to block all attempts at tracing a common pedigree for any animals whatsoever: each case is considered on its own merits.

In the sphere of language, the only part of anthropology that has reached any precision, everything works smoothly: no one doubts that English and Hindustani are of the same stock, though it may not appear at first sight; no one will refuse to consider any reasonable proposal to

Folk-lore, vol. 34, 1923, pp. 224–32.

connect English and Hebrew, but until such a proposal is forthcoming no one will be angry that others decline to believe in their common origin. If you can really prove that Polynesian and Aryan languages come from the same source, so much the better. Distance is immaterial; the rigor of the method alone decides. But can it be that languages, like animals, can converge?

The idea that we express by the verb *to take* is rendered *teku* in one dialect of the Solomons. The two languages are totally unconnected; they have nothing else in common. Is this then a case of convergence? No, because the resemblance has not been brought about by similar conditions. It is pure chance. The number of sounds in any language is limited and coincidences are bound to occur, but they are easily recognized as such and no trained linguist can be taken in by them.

True convergence, however, does occur. Aryan languages express possession by special adjectives called possessives. So does Melanesian, and so doubtless do many other groups. Have they borrowed this peculiarity from one another? If, penetrating below the surface, we examine the structure of these possessives we are forced to deny it. Aryan languages formed their possessives by adding adjectival suffixes to personal pronouns and did so at least four thousand years ago; Melanesian, or its parent tongue, expressed the same idea by particles before pronouns, and this they did at a comparatively recent period. Thus two groups of languages widely removed from one another in space and in spirit, working separately, have arrived at a similar result by different ways; their possessives are in appearance alike, but their structures betray their different origins.

To prove that similar idioms occurring in various languages have a common origin, it is not sufficient to show that the languages as a whole have a common origin, for convergence is especially common among related languages, just as cousins are more likely, in virtue of heredity, to pick up the same habits. Various Indo-European languages have articles that are really unemphatic demonstratives, yet we know that the parent language had none; every schoolboy on the classical side has seen the articles developing in Homer, and knows that Latin had not yet begun to acquire any in the days of Virgil. The curious point is that Sanskrit has independently tended to use as articles the very pronouns that Greek chose for the purpose. The reason is that, being heirs to the same traditions, they have tended to solve the same problems in the same way.

The question that interests us here, however, is whether convergence extends to other creations of the human mind besides language—to art, to customs, to beliefs. We should expect the same laws to inform and pervade all human activities, but such general reasonings are not safe; we want examples.

Architecture supplies us with one. Both Gothic and the Graeco-Buddhistic art of North-Western India possess the trefoliated arch. Does either derive it from the other, or both from a third? The form tells us little, but the structure immediately disposes of the suggestion. First, the Gothic arch is a true arch; the Gandharic is a trabeated arch.[1] Second, we know that the foils of the Gothic arch were produced at first by letting into the soffit of the arches small pieces independent of the moldings; only later were the cusps cut out of the arch. In Gandhara the trefoliated arch was merely the section of a double trabeated dome.[2] Thus two groups of artists, parted from one another by time and space, starting from different principles of construction, arrived at *similar* designs; what they had in common was the artistic feeling that delights in the same forms and is ready to discern them when indicated by the material.

The church of St. Stephen's, Walbrook, supplies us with another instance of convergence: the plan is an octagon of eight pillars supporting a dome and made into a square by the addition of four more pillars at the angles. This is exactly the plan of a Jaina porch.[3] The English and the Indian architect, the one working on the principles of the Renaissance, the other on Indian traditions, have both hit upon the same device for harmonizing a square plan with a circular dome.

The idea of convergence seems to present no more difficulty to the architect than to the philologist, partly because the material is so abundant, partly because he is more conscious of his art as a solution of problems. In sociology, on the other hand, practical experience and theoretic study usually are divorced; the sociologist seldom is a statesman or administrator as well. Social changes, therefore, appear to him as automatic processes, like a stream flowing downhill, not as the constant effort of different races with different traditions to overcome the same obstacles. If, instead of keeping anthropology and European history in watertight compartments, we interpreted the one in the light of the other, the convergence of customs would present no difficulty to the mind.

Feudalism appears in ancient Egypt; it recurs in Europe in the Middle Ages; in Japan recently; in Fiji to the present day. In form these states of society are so much alike that they are described by the same term; but that is no reason for believing that one is derived from the other. The structure of Mediaeval Feudalism shows it to be descended from the Roman Imperial Administration, broken up, usurped, and adapted by barbaric invaders: the titles are the titles of Roman officials with Germanic additions; the bond that unites Europe is the memory of the Caesars. We can find nothing in Fijian feudalism to connect it with ours: titles, ceremonials, prerogatives, religious associations, do not show anything that could be traced to Europe. We do not know exactly what was the state of society out of which Fijian feudalism developed, but it certainly was nothing like the civil administration of the Roman Empire. Yet the process of development was remarkably like the process that took place in Europe: there is evidence that Fiji at one time was more centralized than when it was discovered, and that there had been a king of Fiji; chiefless and ever warring tribes split up his realm into fragments, but adopted much of the style and hierarchy of the country they invaded, only on a much smaller scale. But, just as in the Holy Roman Empire, the old tradition started a process of centralization once more, and already one tribe had attained to hegemony and attempted to revive the kingship of Fiji when we arrested the natural development of Fijian history.[4]

It would appear, then, that feudalism is a stage through which any society accepting the hereditary principle is sure to pass when exposed to disruptive influences, as sure as any mammal will develop horizontally like a fish when it takes to the water. The actual details of the feudal organization will depend on what went before. Once we are in full possession of the facts there can be no doubt whether a resemblance is superficial and due to the convergence, or whether it lies deeper and is the result of a common origin. The caste system of the late Roman Empire and that of India may be related or may merely have converged; the question cannot be decided by a philosophical controversy, but by historical evidence. In the *Hibbert Journal*[5] I translated the thoughts of a Fijian on the decline of his race. The author, inquiring into the causes of this decline, traces it to the neglect of the ancestral gods. He does not, however, propose to dethrone the Christian God in order to reinstate them, but thinks it possible to worship both, the Christian God as a Spiritual God and the Fijian gods as temporal powers; the Fijians should pray to the One for spiritual benefits, to the many for material benefits. "How exactly like the Gnostics," observed one reader, an authority on the Early Christian Church; yet the writer of this essay had never heard of the Gnostics, nor had his teachers: he was merely a zealous Methodist and an equally zealous pagan, anxious to retain the new religion without giving up the old. Perplexed with the same dilemma as the pagan of antiquity he arrived at the same solution, but his doctrine is composed of different materials: his Christianity is not primitive but nonconformist; he calls God Jehovah; the First Person of the Trinity is the most important, and he does not know the sacraments; on the other hand, his paganism is so remote from that of the Roman Empire that if there is any connection it cannot be traced.

As the members of two different groups may converge till they resemble one another, so members of the same group may diverge till only careful study can reveal their original identity. Dugongs and seals would inevitably be classed together by those ignorant of natural history, yet they are but distant relations; their immediate relations are much further removed in appearance from them than they are from one another. Who would imagine at first sight that the dugong is more nearly akin to the ungulates than to the seal? So also in language, the Flemish *pepel* and the Solomon Island *pepele* both mean butterfly and differ only by one letter, yet they have nothing to do with one another. The philologist refuses to identify our word *soup* and the Sanskrit *supa* because he can find no evidence that it is not an accident; on the other hand, who would believe that the Latin *equus* and the Greek *hippos* are one and the same word, seeing they have not a letter in common except the termination? Could anything be imagined more opposed to Mediaeval Feudalism than Roman Administration? Yet the two are more closely related than the various forms of feudalism are to one another.

What then becomes of all our anthropological definitions? The exact meanings of clan, sept, totem, magic, and religion have been debated over and over again, but all these definitions have served only to hamper the progress of historical research. For history is concerned with origins; it is interested to see how one institution gradually changes into another completely different. It is quite otherwise with geometry, which investigates the immutable principles and properties of forms; their definitions are the very foundation of the science, but to introduce them into history is to misconceive its whole purpose and spirit. The result is to bring together those things which are historically unconnected and to keep apart those things which are closely related. We may classify states into monarchies and republics, but by doing so we merely confound all natural relationships. We place the French Republic side by side with the Roman, with which it has little in common but the name and a few pedantic imitations of details that do not matter; we separate it from the British Monarchy, of which it is largely a copy. In many parts of the Pacific Islands each clan reveres an animal which is the incarnation of a god or a ghost, and is therefore called a spirit-animal;[6] these animals can pass all the tests required for admission as totems. In the Solomon Islands, however, Dr. Rivers and I found spirit-animals which are unconnected with any clans and any exogamy and could scarcely pass one of those tests; yet they are obviously the same as the spirit-animals of Fiji and Samoa, only stripped of all those associations which would give them the right to be called totems. On the other hand, anthropologists commonly group together as totems institutions which, for all we know, may have no common origin at all, and which may not even be cases of convergence, but accidental and superficial resemblances. Thus in Fiji we find side by side the spirit-animal and the name-fish of the tribe; the two are quite unconnected in the native mind, and cannot, as yet, be connected by the European mind, for the spirit-animal may not be eaten, while the name-fish is the special food of the tribe.[7] Yet both, according to definitions, should be totems.

There is nothing to be gained by thus joining what should be separated, and separating what should be joined. In the early days of anthropology such groupings were certainly useful. The South Sea Islander's classification of bats with birds and rats with lizards may be convenient for practical purpose, but it fails completely when animals are studied scientifically. So it might have been useful to use the labels *clan,* or *totem,* or *magic* so long as anthropology was merely a curiosity shop of customs; they serve to keep in one's mind vast collections of facts, and introduce a certain order, which is the necessary preliminary to scientific investigation. Men like Tylor performed a very useful function in arranging their collections in such a way that their possibilities could be seen at a glance, that they could suggest problems and stimulate a desire to explain the numberless cases of uniformity in variety by working back to the origins. But once this has become the object of our quest the old classifications must be broken up. All the methods of making fire will no longer be grouped together: the burning glass will be transferred to optical science, from which it is derived; the flint will go to the section of stone implements; and it is a question whether the various ways of making fire by friction may not have arisen independently out of as many different processes of the wood industry, since that would best account for their variety. No longer will magic be put in one case and religion in another, since magic frequently is but debased religion; the spells of the Atharva-Veda will be treated as the continuation of the hymns of the Rig-Veda, while Mediaeval magic will follow its Roman and Germanic antecedents.

The experience of students in other walks of knowledge led us to expect that we should find convergence operating in customs and beliefs. An examination of facts has confirmed that expectation. The examination was worth the trouble, and the time spent upon it has not been in vain, for it will save time in the future. We feel that we can safely disregard henceforth the abstract controversy that centers round the question whether like institutions can have independent origins or not. Convergence undoubtedly exists and common origins undoubtedly exist. The structure of all institutions, when sufficiently known, will point with no uncertain finger one way or the other. There can only be doubt where the evidence is insufficient, and to argue where we do not know is truly unprofitable when there is so much we can know for certain tomorrow, if we choose.[8]

3

Psychology and Ethnology

The ideas of our present generation are so different in many respects from those of our forefathers that we can hardly help believing that our minds also must have radically changed in order to think so differently. In fact, the old ways of thinking are merely being kept in check by accumulated facts and experiments that rise up like walls on the right and left to keep our thought in the straight and narrow path of science, but as soon as a new field of research has been thrown open in which there are no tracks laid out, our thoughts break loose again and range freely and recklessly as of old.

Such is the present condition of ethnology: a playground for speculations escaped from the iron discipline of experimental science.

Larger tomes, volumes of facts, admirable industry in their collation, may give us for a moment the illusion that the present day anthropology has vastly outstripped the methods of Hobbes and Locke. But of all these facts, so patiently and conscientiously collected, only an infinitesimal proportion are made use of in drawing conclusions, only those that square with the theory; we need never read the rest to understand the argument. The method is still that of Hobbes and Locke: given a custom, our first question is, What can have been the intended use of it? Having imagined some use, we postulate the idea of it as the origin of that cus-

Folk-lore, vol. 26, 1915, pp. 115–37.

tom. We thus conclude that the desire for peace and security is the origin of modern government, or a dislike of inbreeding the motive for exogamy. It was and is still the way of rationalistic utilitarian psychology applied to the history of mankind. The curtain used to rise on highly intelligent white men sealing a compact for the abolition of strife; now it rises on a camp meeting of "dull" Australian blacks discussing how to prevent the injurious effects of incest. Religion used to open with philosophical reasonings about the First Cause; now it is content to originate with speculations about natural phenomena.

To explain a custom as the outcome of deliberate invention is to explain nothing. It is taking refuge in an event of which no records can be discovered, and which never can be proved. It is a surrender to ignorance, a confession that it is too strong for us and that the explanation is forever concealed in the dark and intricate mazes of unknown individual minds that vanished from the earth thousands, it may be myriads, of years ago.

But, it may be objected, it is not a question whether this pleases us or not, but whether such things do happen or not. Now it is a fact that men do deliberate and invent things. For instance, a modern novel does not make use of traditional plots; they spring out of the individual mind, according to definite laws, no doubt, and from definite antecedents, but the processes are so complex, the antecedents so numerous, and our clues so few that to trace back the finished novel to all its origins is an impossible task. We can only describe it, therefore, as the work of fancy, which is a way of saying we know not what it is.

The argument, however, is not to the point because the plot of a modern novel is not the creation of a society, nor does it become an institution. As far as the incidents go, the plot is not an ethnological object, because they have their roots in individual experience and do not become incorporated with the culture of the community; they do not become an inheritance of the race; they are forever stereotyped within the covers of a book, ours to read and enjoy, but not ours to appropriate, transform, and hand down so changed to succeeding generations. The plots of a Thackeray or a Hardy are not like the plots of *Little Red Riding Hood* or *Cinderella,* which are still producing pantomimes every year. You can write a history of *Beauty and the Beast,* but not of *Pickwick Papers.*

There are features of the modern novel that are of ethnological interest, such as the treatment of the characters, the moral tone of the plots and their general structure, the neglect or cultivation of style; this we recognize by describing these peculiarities as Georgian, or Early or Mid-Victorian. They are ethnological because they are what some might call the spirit of the times, others the average of all the trends of thought at that period.

It may happen that a knowledge of the actual motives that led up to a political change may mislead the field worker and throw him off the true scent.

In the island of Lakemba, Fiji, the nobility is all descended from Niumataiwalu. It is divided into four clans, which I will call A, B, C, and D. At first we are inclined to connect this fourfold division with the sacred character of the number four in Fiji. But, on enquiring into the past history and the formation of those clans, we find that at one time there were only three, A and C forming one single clan. It was found, however, that the people of A were very slack in preparing for feasts and relied on their cousins of C, who took more interest in public functions, to do all the work and keep up the clan's good name. So it was decided to split off A, so as to throw them onto their own resources and compel them to bestir themselves if they would not be put to shame by making a poor show at festivals. Therefore, we conclude, the fourfold division is a pure accident. Fortunately, however, we do not stop there in our investigations, but go on to other islands, where we find this fourfold division so common that it is evident it once was an institution.

So often is this the case that in the field it is a good rule, after studying minutely one community, to collect bare lists of clans, titles, functions, etc. from neighboring communities in order to determine which features are accidents and which are constant.

Motives arising out of temporary and local circumstances must be temporary and local in their effects. They may for a time be predominant in the minds of the community, but, as soon as they have been satisfied or quashed, their action ceases; but the permanent tendencies are always there. Reasons of state may for a time overwhelm a traditional preference for a fourfold division of the tribe, but this preference will remain when the reasons of state are gone, and it will assert itself at the first opportunity. A chief of C may succeed a chief of C because the candidate of B is unpopular; but at the next election this motive will have disappeared and the chieftainship will return to B. A collective resolution to change a custom, to prohibit incest or whatever it may be, to be permanent must be the outcome of long and steady preparation; show us this preparation, show us previous custom inevitably and logically leading up to the resolution, and we can dispense with the resolution itself, which is to the new order of things but as the guard's whistle to the departure of the train.

Nothing can come out of nothing; a man cannot evolve a whole system out of emptiness. No one has ever denied that Australian blacks do reason, argue, and discuss ceremonies and the application of custom. We do so ourselves, and therefore we can safely assume that savages do likewise without our troubling to go and see. What one is justified in doubting is whether they could evolve a whole social organization out of their own minds. Consider how difficult it is to name a new thing when there is nothing about it to suggest a name; how painful it is to have to find one; how we will rack our brains for days when the whole business could be settled in five minutes by opening a book at random or drawing letters out of a bag.[1] We are in practice thorough determinists: we must have something to determine our conduct, and it must be something of social importance if it is to be accepted by society. Where is the man who would dare name a new island by lottery, and where is the geographer who would accept such a name?

If we worry ourselves to hang even the most trifling inventions on precedents, can we believe that savages, some of the most backward of any we know, can invent a new social order bearing no relation to the old? And if it was founded on the old one, we want to know what that old one was in order to understand the new one.

We are no wiser for being told that Australians deliberated at some time in the distant past, because all men are continually deliberating, only they are not always deliberating about the same objects; it is these objects that interest us by their difference, not their deliberations, which are all very much alike. What we want to know is, What was the state of society, so different from ours, out of which the Australian aborigines evolved another state of society different from the first, and known to us through the researches of Australianists?

The fact that social organization "bears the impress of design upon it"[2] does not prove that it was devised within one day or even a century. The British Constitution "bears the impress of design upon it" to such a point that other nations have copied it; yet it is the boast of every true Briton that his constitution grew and was not made. The truth is, it is being made every day, and is continually being molded by intelligence and design, and a factor that runs so through the whole of history is incapable of explaining a particular episode.

Dual organization does not stop incest in the least. It allows a man to marry his mother, or a daughter her father, depending on whether descent is patrilineal or matrilineal. The natural conclusion is that it was never meant to prevent incest. But the psychological anthropologist prefers the methods of Ptolemy to those of Copernicus. He maintains his original assumption and calls in another assumption to help the first. He supposes that the savage does not think as we do, that if he sets out after a definite purpose he generally goes a roundabout way and often never gets there at all. Thus rationalist, utilitarian psychology has to be supplemented by what we may call functional psychology, which undertakes to explain savage customs by the mental functions of the savage mind: by association, emotion, confusion of thought, massive apprehension, analogical reasoning, and so forth.

Both methods are inconsistent with one another: the first is merely the application of old English psychology to savages and is therefore uniformitarian; the second, on the contrary, is obliged to postulate for the savage different processes of thought to account for his different ideas. This does not prevent them from forming a close alliance. The first concludes that exogamy and matrimonial classes were invented to prevent incest; if you object that there was a much simpler way of doing it by proclaiming, "Thou shalt not marry thy sister, nor thy mother, nor thy daughter," then the second method comes to the rescue with the reply, "Oh, but savages have undeveloped intelligences and could not keep in mind their relationships." After the assertion that savages are no mere machines, but intelligent beings endowed "with a practical ingenuity and logical thoroughness and precision,"[3] it is suggested that this "dull witted savage" found it difficult "to remember his individual relationships with everybody else";[4] that, having definite concepts of mother, sister, and daughter, they could not remember in practice who was who, and had therefore to invent a machinery which failed to work until it had been corrected twice or thrice, and by that time was so "bloated" that it fell into disuse.

I will not dwell further on these inconsistencies. I will merely remark that I have had some acquaintance with savages, and I have never noticed that, like Lamb's Chinese, they burnt their houses down whenever they wanted to eat roast pig.

The application of functional psychology to ethnology need not detain us here, as we shall show further on that the mental operations of a people cannot be deduced from the customs they practice, or their customs deduced from their mental operations.

We will, for convenience's sake, give the name of biological psychology to those theories that explain customs by instincts, real or supposed, of the human mind. The method is much the same as that of the other schools: we begin with a blank tablet, and on this tablet instinct proceeds to write customs. The objections are the same: you cannot evolve something out of nothing; it is impossible to understand how a variety of complex social organizations can in various parts of the world be evolved out of the same bare instinct. Male jealousy is an undoubted instinct, an undoubted factor in human affairs; but how it can have lain dormant for a time, then, according to Lang's theory, suddenly begun to drive out the younger members of the community, and finally quieted down so far as to accept an organized exogamy, is more than has ever been explained. There is in human affairs a postulate of inertia, as in physics: a force that is acting must go on acting, or we must show cause why it should cease; every change of direction or intensity must be accounted for.

If ethnology is to become a science it must postulate that the same cause cannot produce different effects, and that every effect must be fully explained by the hypothesis, or the hypothesis is null and void. If a custom is founded on an instinct it must occur wherever and whenever that instinct is present, or we must be able to point to the cause that is counteracting the instinct. If a custom is founded solely on an instinct, every detail of that custom must be deducible from that instinct.

What should we think of a technologist who explained all the manifold methods of fishing, hunting, and planting by the instinct of hunger? Yet I cannot see that he would be explaining less than a sociologist who would deduce all the varieties of exogamy from sexual jealousy, or the countless forms of totemism from confusion of identity or fear of animated nature.

Even assuming instinct to be at the bottom of all custom, yet that would not help us one atom. For the instincts of man do not form a harmonious body, but a struggling mass of competing impulses, so that even if we could prove that a certain custom is a manifestation of a certain instinct, we should still have to explain why that particular instinct was allowed to come into play at all and was not suppressed by its rivals. And this explanation can only lie in the historical antecedents.

For instance, over the greater part of the world, it would appear, it is the custom for the man to court and propose. The fact seems to require no explanation: it is the law of the animal world for the male to court and the female coyly to assent. And yet in parts of the Solomons it is quite common for the girl to propose: in the Western Torres Straits Islands[5] it is even considered improper for the young man to propose, or to accept the young girl's proposal with too much eagerness. Here, then, the instinct has been completely set at naught, and not by any other instinct that we can think of, but to all appearances by a series of social changes which it is our task to reconstruct by historical research. Instinct in itself appears to be a precarious thing; it is weaker even than etiquette. However deeply in love, an English girl is forbidden by convention to propose; she can only hint in a modest and maidenly way, and, if the hint is not taken,

> Sit like Patience in a monument,
> Smiling at Grief.

But if she is a queen, etiquette requires that she should intimate to the suitor that he is at liberty to propose. South Sea women are not much given to dying of love; a mere liking is enough to overcome female modesty and impel them to propose. That is because custom supports the liking; in England it opposes the strongest passion.

The truth is there is one set of instincts that dominates all the rest, namely the social instincts. Their action is quite indefinite: they are essentially opportunists. They give the whole weight of their support to public opinion; it makes a man care more for what his people think right than for anything under the sun. It is clear that such instincts help us not at all, since they merely reinforce custom, but do not create it.

Instincts, therefore, are useless for our purpose: we can leave hunger out of fishing, love out of marriage,[6] pugnacity out of warfare, religious emotions out of religion, the social instincts out of everything, and man out of ethnology.

We have as yet no use for man, because he is much the same all the world over. There certainly are congenital differences of character between races, and the influence of these differences upon custom may at some future time become an interesting study, when we have first settled the history of these customs; but, in our present state of ignorance, these differences are negligible quantities, and man may be treated as an unchanging quantity. Now, from an unchanging quantity it is impossible to deduce the ever changing and endless variety of custom and belief throughout the world.

The psychological anthropologist will not admit that man is very much the same all the world over: his argument is that different ideas must proceed from different mental constitutions. If that assumption is necessary, then we must assume millions of mental types to account for the millions of different customs and beliefs.

I have never heard it suggested that the contemporary French mind is structurally different from that of two hundred years ago. Yet in those days France was the eldest daughter of the Roman Catholic Church; now the majority are rationalists. We might say without paradox that they are now rationalists because they were once Roman Catholics; the mode of thought is the same: precision, simplicity, logic, and consistency, arguing from axioms rather than experience. It is the axioms alone that have changed.

I have never heard it suggested that the inborn mental constitution of savages is modified by Christianity. In fact there are plenty of Fijians who find it quite possible to be at once heathens and Christians. I have translated a Fijian's defense of heathendom.[7] A Church historian thought it was just the line of argument of the Gnostics. One friend saw in it a parody of contemporary apologetic theology. An old resident in Fiji assumed, as a matter of course, that it was my own invention.

It is precisely because savages think in the same manner as we do that they think different things; for the same processes working on different inherited material must lead to different results, unless we are prepared to admit that $3 \times 2 = 3 \times 3$, or that the same force acting on two different masses will produce the same velocity.

The material upon which the savage mind works is inherited tradition and social organization. We imagine, indeed, that we proceed differently, that we white folk each individually derive our knowledge directly from objective reality, that we believe a thing only because it has objective reality and that we can see it, each for himself. We conclude that our knowledge is rational, objective, and obvious, and we are at a loss to account how the savage can be blind to facts and truths that are staring us in the face; we have to suppose that the eyes of his soul are closed and that he lives in a world of dreams and vague feelings. Men of all races and all generations are equally convinced that they individually draw their knowledge from reality. A savage will defend his beliefs by an appeal to experience, and his doubts as to the sanity of our own are ill concealed, though he is too polite to express them. We think that we believe in atoms because they really exist; a Fijian thinks that he believes in ghosts because he has seen them with his own eyes, and after all if he does claim to have seen a ghost what have we to oppose to the testimony of his eyes but a skepticism which has no reasons but that ghosts do not fit in with European conceptions of the world and are to us an unnecessary hypothesis?

Everyone agrees that savages do not believe in ghosts because they see them, but see them because they believe in them. But it occurs to few to say that we do not believe in our principle of inertia because it is self-evident, but that it is self-evident because we believe in it, or that the economic law of supply and demand is to a great extent created by our belief in it, and not our belief created by the law. Who knows but that a race may sometime arise which has shaken off our mechanical conception of the universe and may proceed to invent psychologies of the twentieth century European to explain how he could possibly be so blind to an obvious and infinitely more fruitful theory of matter and mind? Who knows but that if we could throw overboard our traditional scientific conceptions we could take in vaster conceptions that would embrace mind and matter in one simple system as irresistible as our present mechanics? What we require in studying native customs is more humility, less confidence in the absolute validity of our own systems, and in an intellectual superiority which only seems absolute because, by accident, there is no higher race with which to compare ourselves.

Our physicist does not, every time he wants an hypothesis, make his mind a blank and start again at the beginning; he only tries those constructions which are fairly well in harmony with the traditional physics of the time.[8] Neither does the South Sea islander exhaust every possible combination of ideas in trying to explain some new phenomenon, but draws his theory from the doctrine of spirits to which he has been bred, and which has always proved so fruitful in explanations of every abnormality.

It is a proof of the incorrigible inconsistency of the white man that, on the one hand, we find it necessary to account for the erroneous beliefs of savages by endowing them with a peculiar mind, while on the other hand we give assent, or at least appreciation, to the reasonings of those philosophers and eminent men of science who reduce our own physics to a set of convenient assumptions which experience can neither refute nor confirm, and of simple laws which are approximately verified in experiment and can at any time be superseded.[9] If we remember that our mechanical conception of the world (and I use the word mechanical in a wide and loose sense, to include that impersonal and individualistic conception of human affairs such as we find in political economy), if we remember that this conception is a temporary phase, a tradition which may pass like other traditions, the difference between the savage and the civilized man vanishes. Grant a soul detachable from the body, there is nothing in a South Sea islander's doctrine of ghosts that is illogical or inconsistent with the premises; we cannot refute them by logic, any more than we can an atomic theory. We can only say that there are infinitely more precise and productive hypotheses than a theory of ghosts. If our science does not profess to explain luck as spiritualistic theories do, on the other hand it can explain an infinitely greater number of things better worth explaining and has given us command of the whole earth.[10]

We must in ethnology escape the influence of philosophical systems. They profess to sweep away tradition and preconceived ideas, and to build upon one or two eternal truths. As a matter of fact, they merely rebuild with the old materials, following the old plan but in a simpler style; but of this we are quite unconscious, and imagine that we have come into possession of eternal and immutable truths. We conclude that if a savage does not see them, his mind is defective or, at least, differently made, and we feel it our duty to correct it by telling him that he is wrong and we are right, and he must believe what we tell him or incur our ridicule, the punishment of the Law, or the anathema of the Church.

A savage's mind is anything but defective. He is just a normal social animal whose chief interest in life is his relations to his neighbors. He is quite used to their opinions, he understands them and sees no reason to differ from them. What his neighbor says is plain and fits in with his general views of things and his practical needs; it is vastly more important to him than the obscure and exceedingly dogmatic assertions of the white man, who, besides being an utter stranger and without practical experience of native affairs, manifestly has not a few bees in his bonnet. So far, therefore, from listening to the Voice of Reason speaking through the white man, he has the audacity, if he is a thinker, to deduce his own gods, medicine, chiefs, and birthrate from self-evident truths, even in the style of a European philosopher.[11]

It is as well that the savage does not read our anthropological works, or his peace of mind might be disturbed for ever. Alas! poor savage! Little does he suspect, as he sits cross-legged in his hut, waggling his toes, discussing the yam crop and the weather, getting excited over the description of a monster rock-cod, seeking relaxation in tales that are best translated into Latin, hearing with interest how Mary in a passion left her husband after breaking up every object in the house, listening to John relating how he saw a ghost at dusk and ran away for dear life, discussing the next feast and the morrow's work—little does he suspect what sums of mysticism, of awe, and fear are being placed to his account in Europe. Would he recognize himself in that timorous creature described as ever moving in a world not yet realized, like one continually turning corners into the mysterious Unknown, and as fresh and unused to the game as when he first started a few myriads of years ago?

Let us suppose that a savage of a more curious turn of mind and superior intelligence, having listened to the relations of his traveled friends about European customs and beliefs, should set himself to explain to his countrymen the workings of the European mind. He might write somewhat in the following style:

"With civilized man the bacterio-medical side of everything is always uppermost. When he is at business, or playing, or marrying, he is intensely keen on what he is about. What he is primarily about, however, is to control the process from first to last by bacterio-medical means, so as to be master of health for all time. Just as a dog lives in a world of smells that we cannot perceive, so the white man lives in a world of bacterio-medical infection and contagion that we cannot perceive.[12]

"Everywhere he sees microbes, and germs, and bacilli, disease-bringing agents. He is not even allowed to spit about freely, lest he communicate tuberculosis, as they call it. Our custom of chewing kava is abhorrent to him, and he makes laws to forbid us doing it, thinking it will cause disease. As he will not touch his food with his hands, he has to undergo great inconvenience, using forks and spoons, thus detracting much from the enjoyment of a meal, which is obviously the reason why he eats less than we do. It may be truly said that Fear and Contagion dog him throughout life, and control all his actions. If he but cough, he must cough off the table. Living in such a perpetual state of fear, the community cannot allow the individual to expose himself to contagion that might endanger the existence of all. Hence that extraordinary tyranny of custom we note among them, under which individuality cannot develop. I will give an instance how far this is carried: to convey food to the mouth with a knife is certain ostracism from high society; for the more careful a man is in avoiding contagion the more power he is supposed to have over the bacilli and the greater his prestige and rank. Now to touch the lips with a knife is to run the risk of transferring to them any pollution that may be on the knife. Of course, this is most inconsequent, since the same objection applies to a fork. But the white man does not think logically as we do; he is post-logical. Thus you may see a white man hold a loaf with his hand to cut it, yet he dare not pass a slice with his fingers unless he says, 'Excuse the fingers,' which formula is evidently intended to neutralize contagion.

"Needless to say, the European theory of bacilli does not get at the psychological root of the matter, which is that their highly-strung natures everywhere see the workings of a mysterious power called Contagion, with which the whole world is loaded as with electricity. The theory of bacilli is merely the European way of justifying these feelings."

Here perhaps one of his auditors will interpose: "As for this invisible force, Contagion, or whatever it may be called, pervading things that once were in contact, and operating at a distance, which many civilized men believe in, it is easy to point to facts of experience, light, sound, odor, epidemics, from which it may have been abstracted. But surely so refined a notion cannot lie at the foundation of Bacteriology: we must begin the explanation with some much simpler mental process, which seems to need no further explanation, such as the habit of drawing inferences from analogy. According to contagious medicine thus:

"Latent premise: To touch an infected man communicates disease, therefore, to touch some utensil belonging to an infected man gives disease."[13]

Our savage anthropologist has applied the methods, often the very words, of the psychological school to ourselves. We may admire his ingenuity, but we cannot assent to his conclusions. If the result is unsatisfactory, then presumably the method is also unsatisfactory when applied to savages.

As a matter of fact, savages do interpret our customs psychologically, with results most unfavorable to ourselves. Old Melaia, an experienced midwife and fond of children, once remarked to me that white women did not love their children, for they put their babies into separate cradles that they might sleep with their husbands, whereas Fijian mothers kept their babies by their side on their couch while the husband slept in some other house. I tried to explain that our custom was due to care for the baby lest the mother should crush it in her sleep, and I reminded her of King Solomon's judgment; but as it appeared that Fijian mothers never roll on to their babies, my argument failed. Now, Melaia's argument was quite right as far as Fijian women go; a Fijian mother who put her child away at night would show a lack of motherly love, for a loving mother likes to have her baby always by her side; a Fijian mother who slept with her husband within eighteen months of childbirth must be lustful indeed to fly so in the face of a stringent public opinion. But Melaia was utterly wrong when she argued from Fijian practice to European psychology; a

European mother likes to have the child beside her, but our softer beds and more agitated sleep makes it dangerous to do so, and so loving foresight checks the natural impulse.

An intelligent young Fijian once remarked to me that white men had such an enormous number of taboos to observe. I pointed out to him that we were trained and broken in to observe them from our earliest childhood, and as we grew up got quite to enjoy them. "I understand now," he observed, "I had always thought European children were so harshly treated; I now see the reason why." He, too, had been applying to us the psychological method.

It is because savages interpret our customs psychologically that they think us wicked, or daft, or both.

A customary action is no clue to the state of mind behind it; in our own churches, while the whole congregation is going through the same performance, yet we know that it includes the greatest diversity of temperaments and opinions, and even their present state of mind cannot be inferred from the prayers they are saying, or the hymns they are singing. The sermon, if it is interesting and fixes the attention of the audience, is the only part from which we may infer approximately some of the emotions and thoughts of part of the congregation, precisely because it has features which are not customary.

It is just the same with the savage. Because he is performing a magico-religious ceremony we have no right to infer that the magico-religious side of it is uppermost in his mind.

If there is one mystery fit to strike awe into the hearts of all beholders it is Death. I once saw a dying savage; here we were in the presence not only of Death but of Death's agents, the dread Kita spirits, that had wasted his once powerful frame to mere skin and bones, and left him gasping there, on the threshold of the Beyond, but unable to pass it. Here was food for solemn thoughts; but to them it was only food for impatience. How much longer was he going to be a-dying? He had died once already that morning, but had come to life again and kept them all waiting till he should be ready for his funeral. They got Rakoto to hang some leaves over him to drive away the Kita and let him die, and in the meantime they sat smoking. The leaves apparently took effect; he breathed his last; the women raised the usual wail; he was bundled up, paddled out to sea, and dumped overboard.

If death does not evoke feelings of awe and reverence, perhaps the departure of the soul for the abode of the dead will. Dr. Rivers and I had the good fortune to attend such a departure. We all met together at night in a house. The ghosts came to fetch the deceased away, but they had little to say, except that they had come for that purpose. Kopa was the only one who had any news to give about the future life: he announced, what did he announce? some mystic revelation? No, merely that he and Nui had in the other world bought a boat (presumably the ghost thereof) from the ghost of a white man. But Mamana, his living son, did not appear interested in his father's posthumous business transactions, but bade him begone: "I am a man, you a ghost," said he, "I don't like you. I don't want to speak to you, go away." So that is all we learned that night about the future life.

Perhaps the psychologist will concede that at the present time those beliefs are not accompanied by any strong emotion; but he will contend that these ideas must have had a strong emotional value for those who discovered them. This, of course, is to presuppose that these ideas came into the world quite suddenly, a fact for which we can find no warrant in our own civilization. We develop old customs or invent new ones by carrying existing ideas to their logical conclusion, a process which need not be accompanied by any other emotion but the pleasure of discovery. Vaccination was a boon to mankind, but it does not follow that Jenner was prompted to discover it by a vision of human suffering, or that he had this vision while carrying out his investigations. A discoverer in tropical medicine may think science a blessing to human beings and sing its praises in verse, but it does not follow that he took to medicine out of philanthropy. Does a ritualistic High Churchman necessarily feel mystic emotions while debating the validity of incense, or the apostolic succession? Are his conclusions determined by the amount of mystic emotion each idea arouses in him?

If we are ignorant of the true motives and emotions of our contemporaries and fellow-countrymen, when we have not only the results before us but also their own statements of motives, what hope have we of deducing motives and feelings from a custom invented, the Lord knows where, when, or by whom?

If we had not the hope, neither have we the wish. We can do without it, and have done without it often. The history of art has been doing so for quite a long time. It is true that, wherever possible, it gives the lives of the artists and the occasion of their work; at such times it becomes biography and annals; but where records fail it is forced to become pure ethnology. Especially is this the case in Gothic architecture. There we hear little of architects, but we hear much of styles and periods, of foreign influence and provincial peculiarities, of problems of vaulting and lighting, of their attempted and successful solutions, of the influence of ritual and economic conditions; all these and many more questions can be answered without our knowing by whom a church was built or why.

Already the study of kinship and social organization, having dispensed with Mind, is fast advancing to a high degree of exactness, and Dr. Rivers can already be said to have annexed this province to exact method.[14]

I will not encroach upon territories won by so much patient strategy and faith. I will merely show how even religion is threatened with subjugation, though, as yet, but little impression has been made upon it.

At kava-making in Tonga, food is set down before the chiefs (*'eiki*) by the common people. The chiefs, however, do not eat of it; it is removed by their respective grandchildren and sister's children. The psychologist would say that the chiefs consider it below their dignity to take notice of the food. But where is his evidence that such is their state of mind? If we proceed historically the explanation is a very simple one: we know from independent evidence that the chiefs represent spirits. Now, in making an offering to the spirits, the worshippers offer up the food, which is then removed and eaten. The chiefs are spirits. Therefore, offerings made to them are removed and eaten. Q.E.D. If any one is dissatisfied with this explanation, it cannot be on psychological grounds, for there is nothing in all this contrary to psychological laws.

There is no attempt in this to get at the back of the brown man's mind, and yet we would seem to have proved something, with the hope of proving more hereafter.

Ethnology may be compared to a moving picture, psychology to the operator and his lantern. If a boy wants to know how moving pictures are produced, we expound to him the camera with which they are taken, the lantern with which they are projected on the screen, and the law by which retinal impressions fuse into one continuous sensation. All this mechanism belongs to no particular time or place, but to any moving picture-show at any time in any part of the world, and it is continually in action from the beginning to the end of the film. Improvements may from time to time be made in the machinery, and these will be described in answer to the question why moving pictures are better now than they used to be. When, however, the boy wants to know why the hero of a particular film went up in an airplane, we do not go into the mechanism of the lantern and film, but merely tell him that it was to win the $100,000, without which the hard-hearted father would not allow him to marry his charming daughter. It does not follow that the mechanism does not cause the picture, but only that it is irrelevant.

Let epistemologists explain how it is possible to give two so utterly different and independent accounts of one event, one causal and universal, the other logical and particular, and both independent of one another, the fact remains. We can conceive a psychology of Parliament which would study the frame of mind of M.P.'s under the influence of collective deliberation and traditional party animus; there are histories of debates in which each speech or repartee appears as the logical outcome of preceding statements and situations. A psychology of the stage would investigate the mentality of actors in general, but it cannot explain the particular action of a player at a particular time; that is conditioned by the logic of the play.

The logic of individual conduct is always approximate and unsatisfactory because it is too indeterminate; there is too much chance in it and too much psychology. Two chess players in presence of the same disposition of the pieces may make different moves; we cannot foresee exactly which, though we can expect one, yet whichever is made we can deduce it from the situation and the end in view. It is perhaps a weakness of the historical sciences that in them we are wise after the event. Yet, in the history of a custom, a more rigorous sequence and prediction may become possible within narrow limits, because individual aberrations compensate one another and leave us with nothing but averages to trouble about, because a mass of conflicting psychological processes are eliminated and only a few broad principles remain. Nor are we studying merely the average conduct of large numbers, but that conduct spread over extensive periods of time, during which the fluctuations compensate one another, so that only constant tendencies survive. Each woman may dress differently, but out of all these differences we can abstract fashion. Fashions may vary erratically from year to year, but, if we take a long period, we find a steady progress from the cumbrous, staid, and elderly, to the light, frivolous, and youthful. Our modern records are so full and minute, and they are so near that we cannot see the wood for the trees; but we study savages from a distance which blurs the details, and the absence of records leaves us only the outlines to work upon. That is doubtless one reason why ethnology has begun with savages, instead of beginning, like charity, at home.[15]

If out of all these fluctuations there results in any period of time not a standstill but a continuous progression in one direction, it is evident that there must be some factor or factors at work which are constant in their operation; when they fail we have stagnation. What they may be it will be the task of the future to discover. It is something if, in the meantime, we have determined their direction.

The conflict between psychology and history for the possession of ethnology is not merely a theoretic conflict; it is of the highest practical importance.

The "psychological" point of view logically leads to either of two ways of dealing with natives. They may be described as the "damn nigger" and the "little brown brother" schools. The first lays down that abominable customs presuppose an abominable mind, and, as many native customs are abominable in their eyes, they conclude that dark races are utterly depraved, and are to be treated worse than dogs. The men who hold these views are not necessarily bad men; they are merely logical and narrow in their moral code. We need not stop to refute this doctrine, because it finds little sympathy at home. The other school is more insidious, because it is kinder in intention. They also take custom as an index of character, but, being of a more paternal disposition, they conclude that the native is not responsible for his abominations, that his intelligence and moral sense is undeveloped, and even as a child's. He must be continually supervised, continually told what to do and what not to do, what to think and what not to think, he must be driven as children were driven at school in the good old days, and yet, since he is a child, gross offenses must be but leniently chastised. Here, as it is so often in sociology, theory is father to practice, and savages soon become the children they were supposed to be, and bad children too. To describe the ensuing loss of initiative, of manliness, of common sense and moral responsibility, were too long and sad a tale. Let us hope that a better understanding and appreciation of savage customs will save the survivors from a similar fate.

4

Myths in the Making

In a paper on "The Common Sense of Myth,"[1] I suggested that myths are not the creations of unbridled fancy, but in many cases, at least, are sober historical records. The idea is not new. It is as ancient as Euhemerus, but those who have undertaken to interpret myths as history have themselves indulged their own unbridled fancy, and have drawn entirely on their own imagination in order to reconstruct the original forms, without seeking for guidance among the available facts. They have been content to guess; they have been influenced in their guesses, not by evidence, but by their own preconceived ideas, which, being of a rationalistic turn, have led them to rationalize myths and treat them as allegories. Had they put their trust not in pure reason but in observation, they might have discovered that myths are true in an even more literal sense than they ever suspected.

The examples I quoted in my previous paper were drawn from an unfamiliar part of the world, where an argument is hard to follow because it winds through a mass of strange facts which tend to bewilder. I now propose to use our own Indo-European traditions, and begin with a myth with which almost every schoolboy is acquainted.

The gods of ancient Greece, as we all know, drank nectar and ate ambrosia; that is the common version. But it should be known that they are

Folk-lore, vol. 33, 1922, pp. 57–71.

sometimes represented as eating nectar and drinking ambrosia;[2] Sappho describes how "he brewed a bowl of ambrosia, and Hermes took the flask to act as cup-bearer to the gods."[3] The Greeks, then, believed that the gods ate and drank a substance called ambrosia—that is, "Immortality"—because it was the principle of immortality. "Whatever did not taste of nectar and ambrosia became mortal"; such, Aristotle says in his *Metaphysics,* was the view of the poets; but he, taking the same view as the modern interpreter of myths, treats it as pure invention on the part of the poets: "For," he argues, "how could the gods be eternal, if they needed food?" The poets, however, were right, and they prove to be the better historians; Indian literature bears witness to them.

The ceremonial drink of India was *soma,* and the preparation of it was an important part of Vedic ritual. I need not dwell on a fact so familiar to anyone who has read about Indian religion. I only want to draw attention to one small but important detail. Another common name of *soma* is *amrita,* which means *immortal; amrita* is the same word as the Greek *ambrotos,* of which *ambrosia* is the substantive. It is called the "immortal draught" because, in the words of Prof. A. A. Macdonell, "*Soma* is the stimulant which confers immortality upon the gods. . . . *Soma* also awakens eager thought, and the worshippers of the god exclaim, 'We have drunk *soma,* we have become immortal, we have entered into light, we have known the gods.'"[4] Thus it appears that ambrosia is not a fiction of the poets, but a real beverage which was drunk at the worship of the gods. To the Greeks who had lost the ceremonial it became a myth, but in India it remained a fact.

The words, "We have drunk *soma,* we have become immortal," have usually been treated as mere poetic frenzy, as the boastings of drunken men. But why choose the more difficult explanation, when there is an easier one at hand? The easier one is to take those words literally: the worshippers sincerely believed that by drinking *soma* they became immortal, they became as the gods. The belief that men can and do become gods is one of the most widespread, and it is one that has exerted more influence on human history than any other. Kings are gods over a large part of the world and in many ages; the idea is familiar to all readers of Roman history. Unfortunately, historians have been accustomed to explain the deification of the Caesars as mere Oriental flattery, but a careful study of Egyptian and other Eastern religions shows that it was not more an empty flattery than ambrosia is a mere poetic fiction; it was a real, serious dogma of momentous importance to the world of which it has covered no small part, spreading beyond China and Japan to the islands of the Pacific.[5] India is the last country in the world where we should hesitate to take in a literal sense any claim to be a god. If I were to sum up Indian religion, at least in its later phases, I should say it is deification run to death: it is not only men who are called gods in India. Brahmans called themselves "the Gods of the Earth. At certain times the people prostrate themselves before them in adoration, and offer up sacrifices to them."[6] Every morning he must "imagine himself to be the Supreme Being, and say: 'I am God! there is none other but me. I am Brahma; I enjoy perfect happiness, and am unchangeable.'"[7] The *Satapatha Brahmana* (ii. 2.2), says: "There are two kinds of gods: the gods, of course, are gods; then they who are the Brahmans . . . they are the human gods." Even inanimate objects can become divine when used in ceremonial. The *soma* beverage itself was looked upon as a god; what more natural than that those who partook of his substance should partake also of his divinity.

The *kava* ceremonial of the South Seas may help us to understand the point of view of the Vedic Aryans. *Kava* was prepared in much the same fashion as *soma,* and, in Fiji at least, its preparation was accompanied by hymns. That may not be enough to prove a common origin for both rituals, but it is enough to suggest one, to encourage us to assume one. Anyhow, whether they are related or not, the analogy of one may help us to understand the other. In Fiji at the present day *kava* is drunk freely, as we drink wine, but it was not always so; it is asserted that of old only the chiefs drank of it. Now the chiefs, as I have shown elsewhere, were divine. Therefore, it may be said that the gods drank *kava*. Furthermore, *kava* is the central point of the installation of the chief, so much so that a new chief not yet installed was said "not yet to have drunk"; until he had drunk he did not assume the title, which sometimes was the same as the god's. Hence we may infer that by drinking *kava* a chief became a god. This inference is confirmed by the use of *kava* in the spiritualistic cult that has recently arisen. Four of us took part in the initiation once: the *kava* was prepared and prayed over, then we drank, and then we became possessed by spirits of that kind known as "water-sprites." After this ritual the medium said I must have a shrine for my own familiar spirit, Lindinaasease by name, who had thus entered me; he anointed a stick of mine with *kava,* so that it became the abode of the spirit, who dwells there (as I hope) to the present day. And here we have another point of resemblance between *kava* and ambrosia, for ambrosia also was used as an ointment. Homer describes how Hera "with ambrosia first from her desirable body cleansed all stains."[8] It does indeed look as if *kava* were after all but a substitute for *soma,* or both substitutes for the same original substance, for substitutes were known even in those days. The modern *soma,* for instance, is not the same as the ancient one, but a substitute. However that may be, whether the Vedic or the Fijian ritual have their roots in the same original ritual or not, we are, I think, justified by the analogy in concluding that the gods of the forefathers of the Greeks and of the Indo-Aryans incarnate in kings and priests used to partake of a beverage called *immortal,* because it renewed their immortality. Hesiod and the poets were right in saying that the gods drank ambrosia, because they did.

I have not yet done, however, with this myth: I should like to trace a recent development of it. Mr. Walter Leaf in his note on *Iliad* 2. 19 argues that as ambrosia always means fragrant, in Homer, it may be derived from the Semitic *amara,* which means *ambergris.* It will seem strange to treat a scholar's gloss as a continuation of myth building; we are so accustomed to assume that the creation of myths involves mental processes that have nothing in common with the inferences of scholars. Personally, I can see no psychological difference between Mr. Leaf's suggestion and an etymological myth such as the following from Fiji.

Etymological myths are very much in fashion now in Fiji, or were so ten years ago. They are multiplied indefinitely by the adherents of neo-paganism,[9] whether imitated from the Bible or suggested by ancient precedents I do not know. Anyhow, they are manufactured freely to explain the names of localities and grafted into the legend of the Flood and the Dispersion.[10] One has been devised for the island of Moala. The name of that island is not Fijian, but Polynesian; the myth-maker, therefore, corrects it to Muala, asserting that it was changed to Moala by the Tongans who overspread that part at the beginning of the nineteenth century. He tells how one party of those who were dispersed at the flood went searching for a new home and sighted some islands. "Which shall we steer for?" they asked their chief. "*Ki mua la* (Bowwards ho!)," he answered; hence that island was named Muala. The philologist will reject this etymology at sight; besides, the name of Moala is found in the distant island of Rotuma under circumstances that suggest that the name existed in that form long before the Tongans invaded Fiji. We who are trained in the comparative method, who have the patience, the time, and the funds to prosecute research over large areas, have discovered that part of Fiji was Polynesian before it was Fijian, and we can explain the form Moala as a relic of the Polynesian occupation; but the author of this episode was ignorant of the fact. He thought of the islands as vacant until his people settled there; he had to explain the Polynesian form of the name, so he explained it in the only way open to him, as a recent Tongan corruption. Restoring what he took to be the original form of the word, he analyzed just as a modern philologist might do, only without his training; this analysis and the example of other stories suggested to him the little episode I have related. In the same way Mr. Leaf, unacquainted with the worship of divine kings, can make no sense of an "immortal draught" and concludes that this is a false derivation; he then traces the word *ambrosia* to a Semitic root which gives a commonplace explanation. One explanation we called a myth, because it is inserted in what would usually be called a myth, and because it takes the form of a story; the other we call a comment, because it stands at the foot of a page under Homer's text and because it involves no picturesque events. But the mental processes are the same: both the Englishman and the Fijian have lost the tradition which is the key to the problem. Like anyone else they are worried by any fact that stands apart and will not fall into their general scheme of things, and, like everyone else, in default of a natural explanation which gently absorbs the fact they will push it and squeeze it till it fits into a place that is not meant for it. In both cases we have loss of meaning, resulting in a totally new meaning; where they differ is in their ideas of evidence and in the latitude which they consider they may lawfully allow to their imaginations.

Loss of meaning and consequent misconstruction play a great part, I believe, in the building up of myths. I do not say the sole part; I am not concerned here with the processes that may conceivably have helped to produce myths, but only those which can be definitely proved to have taken part. I have often been asked, "Don't you think myths may have arisen in this way, or in that way?" But I am still waiting for examples, and until examples are forthcoming it is fruitless to discuss these supposed ways in which myths may arise. You can do so much with a "may" that there ceases to be any fun in the game; it is far more amusing to trace what actually did happen. Now loss of meaning is one of the things that has happened, and pretty often too. We can readily see why, for customs continually are decaying, and with each one that passes away the meaning of some old tradition is lost, for a narrative always assumes that certain customs, or beliefs, or events are known to the audience. The speaker cannot stop at every turn to expound them; he takes them for granted, but it sometimes happens that the knowledge he presupposes is wanting, because he is speaking to a generation or a people that does not possess his experience. Then misunderstandings arise, as constantly happens when Europeans attempt to explain to savages things of which they have not the remotest conception; the same happens when savages tell things to Europeans who are not sufficiently acquainted with their customs.

I will give an instance from my own experience, for I very nearly became, quite unwittingly, the author of a miraculous legend, not by giving a free rein to my fancy, but on the contrary, while I was conscientiously trying to record as accurately as possible the manners and customs of Eddystone Island in the Solomons. I was noting down the legend of the Flying Chief, who was killed by the people of Pou and Lape because he had concealed from them a new type of fish hook with which he caught ten or twenty bonitoes to their one. His own people carried his body inland to bury him. Arrived at a certain spot they asked, "Will this do?" "No," he answered, "the Pou and Lape killed me, and they are not far."

They carried him to Inusa: "Let us leave him here," they said, but he objected because Pou and Lape were in sight. At last they found a spot where Pou and Lape were out of sight, and then he assented.

Now I will wager that most of my readers in hearing the narrative have understood that the dead man raised his voice and uttered the words ascribed to him. That is exactly what I understood at first, and would have continued to imagine if I had been interested only in stories and never troubled about the customs. I should then have come home and propagated my error; possibly the legend might have been quoted by other students as an instance of the dead speaking. Fortunately, I had pursued my researches sufficiently far to discover my error. It occurred to me that the natives constantly conversed with ghosts by means of divination: a man would hold a shell-ring at arm's length and then question the spirit, who answered by making the arm whirl round and round. This was commonly spoken of as "talking with the spirit." Dr. Rivers and I have seen it done time and again, and the natives probably still talk with ghosts at the present day, unless they are now Christianized. Thus, what appeared at first a miracle turns out to be the most commonplace affair, so commonplace that a native story-teller would not need to go into any explanations, but only just report the conversation between the ghost and the living, and his hearers would immediately understand how it was carried on. But let a stranger hear it who has never talked with spirits and he will necessarily construe it as a miracle, and turn into a wonder what is really a plain tale which might well be true in every detail.

This example should teach us how frequent such interpretations must be, and how numerous must be the myths scattered among the writings of scholars discoursing on ancient literary remains which assume in readers a knowledge we no longer possess.

Loss of meaning and new interpretations are by no means confined to myths. They are familiar to every student of language. For example, the Latin preposition *tenus,* "as far as," originally was a noun in the accusative, and as long as it was felt it governed the genitive; but when it became obsolete, except in this use it was mistaken for a preposition and took the ablative.[11] The word *tenus* once was a living noun; its accusative formed part of a complete system, or declension. But when that system broke down, the accusative used as a preposition was left an unattached vagrant; it had to be adopted into a different family of words in order to become intelligible, and on being so adopted it assumed the style of its new relations. Mrs. Wright's fascinating book on *Rustic Speech and Folk-Lore* contains several instances of this process.[12] Take the word *geometry,* for instance; no one who has learnt the subject can mistake the meaning. So long as there are people acquainted with both, so are form and sense preserved intact generation after generation; tradition helps our memories by making us understand. But let the word fall among rustics to whom that classical tradition and scientific experience are unknown, and it straightway becomes adapted to the ear and the knowledge of country folk; it is spelt *jommetry* and means *magic*. In this new form and sense it becomes stable, because it is in harmony with the traditions of its new home. The knowledge of a few keeps the word *polyanthus* from going astray among the educated classes; but when it reaches people who are not under the influence of those few it becomes *Polly-Andrews* or anything that is in keeping with the English language and English ideas. In the same way *bronchitis* becomes *brown-typhus* to those who have never heard of *bronchia*. Sometimes a word is kept unaltered by sheer effort of memory, no one being able to account for the outlandish form, or not enough people to affect even the cultivated class; shame alone preserves the word, everyone fearing to lose caste by mispronouncing or misspelling. Thus it is with the word *asparagus;* it would be more picturesque and more interesting, and it would economize our memories, if we could call it *sparrow-grass,* but we dare not for fear of being assigned to the lower classes.

The reason for these changes is that words, like all other ideas, cannot live in isolation, but only as parts of a system. They must conform in sound and in sense with the general spirit of the language. If they do not they tend to perish; they must conform in order to survive. If, therefore, a word for some reason or other breaks loose from the constellation to which it belongs it must get lost, unless it can attach itself to some new constellation, and to do this it must suffer change. There may be a few exceptions, as I have mentioned; isolated cases may be artificially kept in being, but these cases are few or the strain on the memory would be too great. One need not have studied experimental psychology to know what a strain it is to remember any disconnected matter. Nonsense syllables, figures, words strung together without rhyme or reason—everyone has some time or other tried to remember such strings of words by weaving them into a story or embedding them in mnemonic verses.

It is a constant tendency of man, therefore, to invest with meaning the meaningless, if for some reason or other it has to be remembered. We shall realize the strength of that tendency when we consider the volumes and volumes that have been devoted merely to the clearing up of obscure but precious texts.

The history of arts reports similar occurrences. Everyone will be able to think of instances. I will just give one. The Buddhist mound, or *stupa,* was a dome surmounted by a staff bearing parasols. On coins it is represented by a half-circle with a vertical line on the top for the staff, but this line has been prolonged through the half-circle, and the whole has been mistaken for a bow and arrow.[13]

The amount of imagination required to invest with a new meaning a story that has become meaningless varies greatly. It is never wholly absent, for in listening to anyone we are hard at work thinking all the time and constructing a mental picture from the hints he conveys to us, for in speaking we never exhaust all the details; that were impossible and unnecessary, but we merely indicate the essentials and the hearer does the rest. Even in the case I have quoted from my own experience, my misunderstanding of the Legend of the Flying Chief, there was some sort of reasoning. I had to interpret the expression "talking with the dead," and in order to do so naturally drew on what I had heard or read in the past. I remembered Lazarus and whatever cases of resurrection may be told in books. I was striving, however, to keep my own mind out of play as much as possible; where there is no such preoccupation the interpretation may be far more elaborate. In the etymological myth of Moala the myth-maker has invented a whole episode for which tradition gave him no warrant; his imagination, however, was not working entirely in the air, as myth-makers invariably are assumed to have done, but he was merely following existing models.

Prehistoric men are always credited with an abnormal degree of fantasy; they are commonly represented as evolving the most elaborate myths out of their own consciousness without any reference to tradition. When a myth explains a custom or something in nature, it is concluded straightway that the myth was constructed entirely to meet the case. No positive proof is ever brought forward, but we can sometimes prove the contrary. The late Mr. Vincent Smith says that the *Citralaksana* "relates a pretty legend of the manner in which the art of painting originated, the substance of which is that the god Brahma taught a king how to bring back to life the dead son of a Brahman by painting a portrait of the deceased, which was endowed with life, and so made an efficient substitute for the dead boy whom Yama refused to give up." Not so very long ago we might have thought this story had been invented on purpose to explain the origin of painting, and called it an "etiological myth," but we now know that statues and paintings originally were not mere ornaments, but habitations provided for the spirit of a god or of a deceased person.[14] The myth, therefore, was not composed to explain the origin of painting, but merely records its true origin; the details may be wrong, but the substance is true. In most cases, however, the myth does not contain the true explanation; we refuse to believe that the scarcity of soil in the island of Kambara in Fiji was due to the god throwing it down anyhow in a fit of temper, instead of spreading it carefully. Yet it would be rash to conclude that the legend was devised on purpose to explain the barrenness of Kambara. In "The Common Sense of Myth," I showed that, on the contrary, it is based on a fact, on the custom of carrying the sacred soil on migrations and on the actual carriage of this soil from the mainland to Kambara, and that the story was afterwards used to explain a fact of nature, and was not invented for the purpose. Where such a procedure differs from ours is that we should never think of using a fact of human history to explain a fact of geology; but then our training has been different, and also our capacity for impersonal reasoning is much greater.

Let us return to the origin of painting. There is one detail which obviously does not correspond to fact and is a later addition, namely the god Brahma's part in the story. This is but another example of that economy of memory which takes such a large share in modifying traditions; there is a limit to what a man can conveniently carry in his head, but tradition is always accumulating. It is necessary, therefore, to simplify the old in order to make place for the new; names are especially hard to remember, and so drop out faster than the episodes in which they figure; the tendency, therefore, is to refer all deeds of note to one or two mighty personages that stand forth among the more obscure crowd. The Hindus traced all inventions to Brahma. The Buddha attracted to himself all the fabled actions not only of men but of animals, thanks to the doctrine of transmigration, which gave him innumerable lives to fill with action. No one in Europe has succeeded in making such a corner in history, yet the Devil has appropriated a great deal in the region of the marvelous and Cromwell in sober history. I need not insist on an occurrence which is familiar to every student of folklore; I only mention it because I have undertaken to point out some of the processes known to play a part in molding tradition, in the hope that others will contribute some more which they have discovered by a careful study of facts.

There are two ways of proceeding in this study. One is to use the historical material that is available. A myth is examined in its successive forms, and from the results we infer the causes. The other is to catch myths actually in the making, either by observation or by experiment, as Mr. F. C. Bartlett has done in *Folk-Lore* for 1920.* The two methods are not as different as may seem at first sight, for in both cases we have only the starting point and the finishing point; we must bridge the gap by inference, for we cannot look into people's brains and see what actually happens, but in the second method those gaps are much smaller and the conditions are better known. For the experimental treatment I must refer to Mr. Bartlett's article; it must be remembered, however, that there are conditions which experiment cannot reproduce, such as the pride of old traditions, political or religious bias, and many other influences which affect myths, as well as any other kind of history. I have quoted one case of observation from my own experience. There is one process which is comparatively easy to observe, because it is so glaring, and that is the falsifying of tradition; I have known no fewer than four of these makers of legend, including the author of the Moala myth. It is interesting to note that none of them were sound, healthy individuals; unfortunately, I was not interested in the matter at the time, and I did not study them closely enough to be able to describe accurately their mental types, beyond labeling them more or less abnormal. It remains, however, to be seen how far these myth-makers, whether downright liars or merely irresponsibles, really affect tradition; their versions certainly do not meet with ready acceptance in a community which is keenly interested in its own history and eager to keep pure and unadulterated the traditions handed down by its forefathers; among savages there is as great a zeal for historical truth as anywhere. But it is possible that when the interest in traditions dies out with the breakdown of old customs, forgeries gain readier credence. That is what seems to be happening at the present day in Fiji; the young generation schooled with a bastard European schooling are like houses swept clean of old and venerable superstitions, and left open to new and unwholesome impostures.

There are interesting lines of research which I can recommend to those who dwell among peoples to whom myths are still as real as the Norman Conquest is to us.

Much, indeed, remains to be done in this sphere. Language has had its share of attention, and so has art. It is time now that those feelings and ideas which, never embodied in metal or stone, live in the mind alone, should be acknowledged as realities as real as those that can be touched and capable of being treated with the same rigor as anything that falls under our senses.

5

The Indo-European Kinship System

In 1889 B. Delbrück published in the *Abhandlungen der philologisch–historischen Klasse der königlichen Sächsischen Gesellschaft der Wissenschaften* a most exhaustive study of the kinship terms in use among people speaking Indo-European tongues. Since then exploration, and especially the admirable researches of Rivers and of Kohler, have considerably altered our point of view, and this must be our excuse for setting out with a very meager knowledge of those languages and their literature to revise a treatise of as much erudition as Delbrück's.

Delbrück does not definitely answer the question of to which type the system used by the speakers of the original European tongue belonged. He does not discuss its relation or its interaction with that very widespread and important neighboring system known as the cross-cousin system. Yet that system has so contested the ground with the invading system as to prevail among at least one people of Indo-European tongue, namely the Sinhalese.

It is to these questions we particularly wish to devote our attention in this paper, but before we proceed to our facts it is well to repeat a few generalities for the sake of those who are not familiar with the study of kinship.

The kinship systems now in use among European peoples of Indo-European speech belong to a type which, since Morgan, has usually been known as descriptive. The term, as Rivers has pointed out, is rather

Ceylon Journal of Science, sec. G, vol. 2, pt. 4, 1928, pp. 179–204.

unfortunate because the terms used in these systems do not describe anything at all. The word *brother,* for instance, does not describe the relation of a man to the son of the same parents; it is just a technical term, of which the meaning has to be learned. If we called him "father's son," then we should be using a descriptive expression. Rivers proposes to call ours and related systems the family system because it is based on the family as conceived in Europe, that is, a group consisting of a living couple and their descendants. It might also be called the individual system because it centers round an individual: it is characteristic of it that no two persons apply the same term to every one of their relations. Thus two brothers, Peter and Paul, have the same father, same mother, uncles, aunts and so forth, but Peter's wife and children are not Paul's wife and children. It may at first seem ridiculous to suggest it could be otherwise, yet we shall see that it is otherwise in the classificatory systems.

The term *classificatory* is again unsatisfactory, since all kinship systems are classifications. Yet the term has become so well established that it might as well be retained, especially as it is not quite as unsatisfactory as the term *descriptive*. What the early students meant to express was that in this system relations are divided into extensive classes, in contrast to the family system, in which a term is applied by one man only to one person, or two, or, at most, a few. Thus, according to our reckoning, a man has only one father, one mother, two grandfathers, two grandmothers, and a limited number of uncles, aunts, and children. The Dravidian, Melanesian, and many other races, on the other hand, speak of the begetter as but one of a large group who are all called fathers: the father's brother is a father, and it follows that your father's brother's father's son, being your father's brother, is also your father, and so on. Peter's wife and children are also his brother Paul's wife and children, and even his cousin John's, because John as father's brother's son is a father's son, and therefore a brother. Thus, out of the terms a Dravidian or Melanesian applies to his kinsfolk you could never construct a genealogical tree, as you can more or less out of our system, which could thus aptly be described as the genealogical system. The classificatory system might also be described as the collective system because no relationship is peculiar to one man, but every one of his kinsmen is related in exactly the same way to a whole set of people as to himself. The essence of the collective system might be expressed mathematically thus:

	Ego	= brother;
∴	Ego's son	= brother's son;
∴	Ego's wife	= brother's wife.
	Father's brother's son	= brother;
∴	Ego's son	= father's brother's son's son;
	Etc.	

So ingrained is this collective point of view where the system is unaffected by other systems that men will commonly speak of "our mothers" or "our wives."

Within the genus classificatory or collective there are several species. One of them calls all relations in the same generation brothers and sisters, all those in the previous generation fathers and mothers, and so on. But in another species, known as the cross-cousin system, relations fall into two groups: in one group are all those who are related through people of the same sex, namely the father's brother, the father's brother's son, the father's father, and father's mother, the mother's sister, mother's sister's son, and so on. Within that group terms are applied exactly as in the simple classificatory system first mentioned: those in the same generation are brothers, in the previous generation fathers, and so on. We shall call these relationships straight. The other group consists of persons related through people of opposite sexes; father's sister, father's sister's son, mother's brother, mother's brother's son, mother's father, and so on. All the members of the straight group go back to the relation of brother-brother or else sister-sister; the second, or crossed, group is based on the relationship brother-sister.

Such are the three systems of which we must grasp the principles before we can proceed to trace the original form of the Indo-European system and its interaction with systems that it has displaced or that have displaced it. A few characteristic relationships in the form of a diagram will show best their differences.

A. Individual

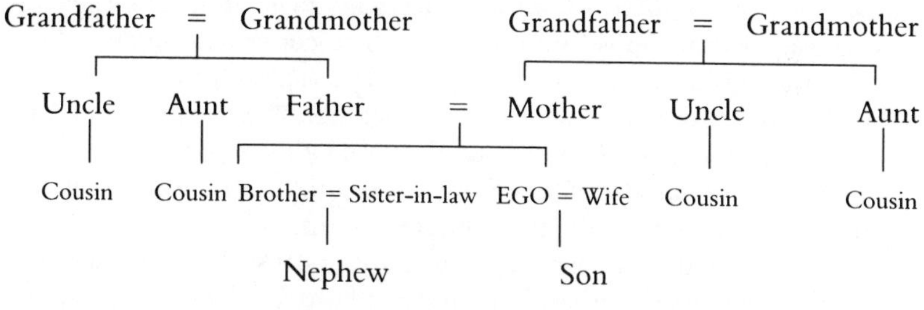

B. Simple Classificatory

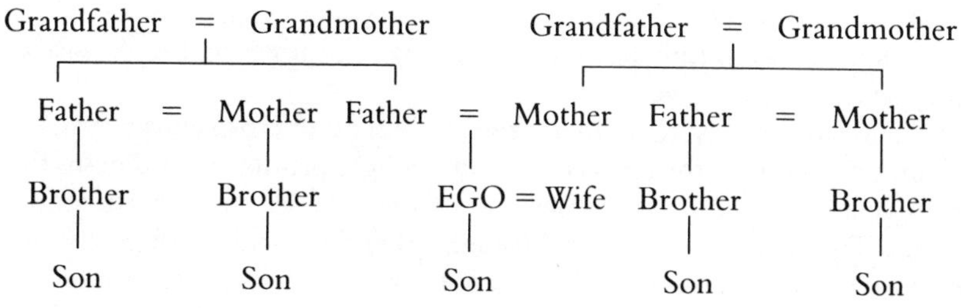

B 2. Cross-cousin

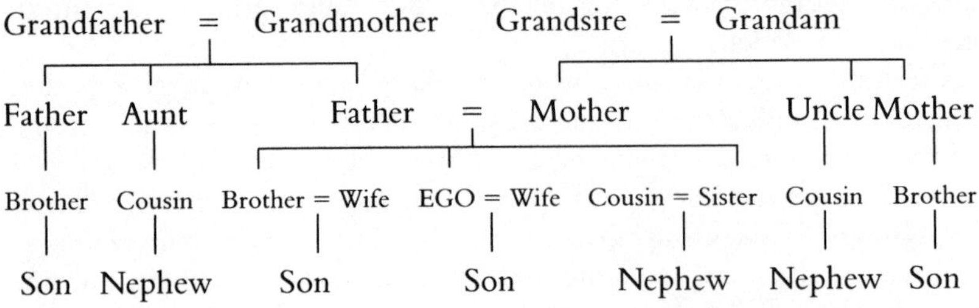

Let us begin our review of Indo-European kinship terms with that furthest eastern outpost of Indo-European languages, Ceylon.

I. Sinhalese System[1]

The general term for a relation is *nädäyā* (both *ä*'s long), from Sanskrit *jñāti*.

A. STRAIGHT RELATIONSHIPS

Sahōdarayā, this is Sanskrit which has displaced the old Sinhalese *sohoyuru, sohovuru* derived from *sahodara*. The word etymologically means "of the same womb," yet in Ceylon it has been extended to the father's brother's son, the father's father's brother's son's son, the mother's sister's son, the mother's mother's daughter's daughter's son, and any one who is *sahōdarayā* to one of these; in short, it covers any male of the same generation whose relationship is "straight." It will be convenient in describing this and other classificatory systems to translate *sahōdarayā* and equivalent terms by our word *brother,* and by the expression *own brother* to indicate that the term under discussion is used of a brother in our sense of the word. The word *sahōdarayā* is of learned origin and is not commonly heard. Ordinarily, one of the two following terms is heard.

Ayiyā, from the Sanskrit *ārya,* worthy, means elder brother, not merely the own elder brother, but anyone who is an elder brother in the classificatory system. In literature one meets with the term *bä* (*ä* long), from Sanskrit *bhrātar.*

Malli, in literature *mal,* means younger brother in the classificatory sense.

The Sinhalese system differs from certain other cross-cousin systems insomuch as it uses the terms elder and younger brother according to the relative ages of the two kinsmen. That is not the case in other regions, such as Fiji: there, in the case of brothers other than own brothers, the use of the terms depends not on the ages of the persons referred to, but on the ages of the own brothers through whom they trace their relationship.

Thus a Fijian boy of the senior branch is reckoned as the elder brother of an adult of the junior branch.

Sahōdarī is the feminine of *sahōdarayā*. It means sister, father's brother's daughter, mother's sister's daughter, and any woman of the same generation whose relationship is straight. This term is not common, but is becoming more so. Ordinarily one hears one of the following terms:

Akkā: elder sister; it also is used in addressing an elder brother's wife, notwithstanding that this is really a cross relationship.

Nangi, nagā, naňgā: younger sister; Prof. W. Geiger connects it with Sanskrit *nagnā,* a girl that has not reached puberty.[2]

Here again the Sinhalese system differs from others that are more thorough-paced in basing their systems on the distinction between descendants of relatives of the same sex and descendants of relatives of opposite sexes. Those systems have no word which always, like our word *brother,* applies to a male, or always, like our word *sister,* applies to a female. The word for a man's brother also means a woman's sister, and a different word is used to include both a man's sister and a woman's brother. This classification is based not on absolute but on relative sex: a man is not always a brother, but is a brother to a man, a sister to a woman. As the opposition of the sexes lies at the foundation of the whole cross-cousin system, it would seem that this usage is the original one, and that the Sinhalese have departed from it under the influence of Indo-European usage.

Piyā, from Sanskrit *pitar,* is used only in polite society, and then only in the third person for a man's own father. The colloquial terms are *tātā, appocci.* The father's "brothers," if older than the father, are known as *loku appā, loku appocci, loku tātā,* that is, "great fathers"; if younger, they are called *bāppā, bāppocci.* The mother's elder sister's husband also is called "great father," and her younger sister's husband *bāppā.*

Mav, "own mother," is from Sanskrit *mātar,* and the same is true of it as of *piyā.* The term *mäṇiyandä* (both *ä*'s long) is used only in address. The common term is *ammā,* which also is used in addressing any elderly woman. *Ammaṇḍī* is a term of endearment. The mother's "elder sisters" are *lokuammā,* her "younger sisters" *bālammā, puňciammā, kuḍammā,* little mother. The father's elder brother's wife also is a great mother, and his younger brother's wife a little mother.

Muttā (Galle), *sīya* (Colombo), and *āta* (Colombo) mean grandfather, grandfather's "brothers," and, in fact, any relation in the third generation up.

Āttā, ācci (vulgar), *miti* (classical) mean grandmother, grandmother's sister.

In the matter of grandparents the Sinhalese system again has fallen off from the consistent cross-cousin system, which distinguishes between a father's father and a mother's father, between the mother's mother and the father's mother. I call such systems consistent because the two grandfathers belong to opposite groups, the man's and the wife's, as do the two grandmothers to the wife's and to the man's. This feature must therefore be original, and the confusion between both kinds of grandparents indicates a breakdown of the two-group systems.

Generations above grandfather and grandmother are called *mīmuttā* and *miāttā*.

Putā, Sanskrit *putra:* son, man's brother's son, woman's sister's son.

Dū, Sanskrit *duhitar:* daughter, man's brother's daughter, woman's sister's daughter.

Munuburā: grandson, brother's grandson, any male relation in the grandson's generation. Prof. Geiger connects it with Sanskrit *manorama,* "pleasing to the mind."

Minibirī: feminine of the above.

B. CROSSED RELATIONSHIPS

The general term for crossed relationships is *ävässa.*

Massinā: mother's brother's son, father's sister's son, and anyone who is their brother; also wife's brother, sister's husband.

Nänā (long *ä*): feminine of *massinā.*

As in the case of brother and sister, so in these crossed relationships the Sinhalese use these two terms according to absolute, not relative, sex. A Fijian man would call a man *massinā,* a woman *nänā* (long *ä*), but a Fijian woman would do the reverse.

Māmā, in literature *mayilā,* from Sanskrit *mātula:* mother's brother, and anyone who is a brother to him.

Nändā, or more respectfully *nändammā,* from Sanskrit *nandinī, nanandar:* father's sister, and anyone who is a sister to her; wife's mother, and anyone who is a sister to her.

Bänā (long *ä*), Sanskrit *bhāgineya:* man's sister's son, woman's brother's son, daughter's husband. The term is translated cross-cousin.

Lēli: man's sister's daughter, woman's brother's daughter, son's wife.

The system is based on the rule that a man should marry his cross-cousin, that is, mother's brother's daughter or father's sister's daughter. The rule is still commonly followed in Ceylon. Such a union makes the maternal uncle the father-in-law, the paternal aunt the mother-in-law. Quite consistently, therefore, the same term is used for the mother's brother and the wife's father, for the father's sister and wife's mother. If we work it out we shall find that under such a rule all the relations by marriage are crossed relations also, so that there is no need for special terms for in-laws. In places where the cross-cousin marriage is in full swing we find that there is only one set of terms for both; thus the term cousin applied to a person of the same sex means also a brother or sister-in-law; if applied to a person of the opposite sex it means also wife, uncle = father-in-law, and so on. But the Sinhalese system no longer is pure; society no longer rests on cross-cousin marriage, and there may be relations by marriage that were not related before the marriage. We find accordingly a set of terms for in-laws such as should not occur in a rigorous cross-cousin system.

C. RELATIONS BY MARRIAGE

Puruṣayā is borrowed direct from Sanskrit, where it means man, male. *Svāmiyā* also is Sanskrit and means "lord, master." Both are used for husband but rarely. Sometimes a woman will speak of *magē mahatmayā,* "my gentleman." Low class women sometimes will say *minihā,* a man. As a rule, however, a woman will speak of her husband, as other people do, by his title, e.g., the schoolmaster, the postmaster. If there is a child a wife will call her husband the father of her children, e.g., *Poḍinōnāgē tāttā,* Podinona's father.

Hāminē from Sanskrit *svāminī,* mistress: wife. She also is called *gedara ätto* or *ätta,* the owner of the house, from Sanskrit *asti,* to be. (The common word for woman, female, is *gäṇi* (long *ä*) from Sanskrit *gehinī,* mistress of the house.) The word I most often have heard is *pavla,* which means properly "wife and children," but has come to mean "wife." If a mother, she is also known as "the mother of So and So." The wife is often the husband's *nänā* (long *ä*).

Suhurubaḍu is from *suhuru,* which is the same as *sohoyuru,* brother, and from *baḍu,* a word of unknown meaning, and means a brother-in-law. It occurs in the Rājavaliya and Pūjavaliya,[3] but is not now in use.

Suhul is the Sanskrit *svasru,* mother-in-law. It has never been given to me when I have collected the terms applied to various individuals.

Bäḍä (second *ä* long) is purely a literary term for the brother's wife, and is applied to any stranger's wife. It is never used of the father's sister's daughter or mother's brother's son. Mr. Paranavitane analyzes it as a compound of *bä* (*ā* long), brother, and *dä* (long *ä*), wife, from Sanskrit *jāyā,* but Prof. Geiger traces *dä* to *jāti,* kind, class.

The Vädda system as given by Dr. and Mrs. Seligman in their *Veddas* is the same as the Sinhalese. The terms are the same, except, of course, for the absence of learned words. The term *hūrā,* cross-cousin, which is a literary word in Sinhalese and rarely heard, apparently is the common Vädda term. It is from Sanskrit *svasurya.* In the same way the Väddas use the *yēli* contracted form of the literary Sinhalese *yeheli* for *lēli,* man's sister's daughter. *Yēli* means properly a female friend, and is so used in ordinary Sinhalese.

Of the twenty Vädda terms given by the Seligmans, seven are known to be of Sanskrit origin and three have been traced with great probability to Sanskrit words. This is only one of many facts that prove that whatever they may be in their mode of livelihood, in their customs the Väddas are not primitive.

The cross-cousin system, as illustrated by Sinhalese usage, extends over the South of India. The overwhelming majority of its adherents, therefore, are people who speak Dravidian, not Aryan. It will be useful, therefore, to set beside the Sinhalese terms those used by the Tamils of the North of Ceylon.[4]

II. Tamil System

The general terms for relations are *suṟṟattār, iṉattavarkaḷ, iṉañcanam.* The last word contains the Sanskrit *jana,* kind.

A. STRAIGHT RELATIONSHIPS

Sagōdaraṉ from Sanskrit *sahodara* is used of brothers in general, older or younger, but only by learned people. In ordinary speech the following two are used:

Aṇṇaṉ: elder brother, father's brother's son, if older, like Sinhalese *ayiyā.* The eldest brother is *mūttaṇṇaṉ* or *periyaṇṇaṉ.*

Tambi: younger brother.

Brothers who are what we should call first cousins can be distinguished from own brothers by calling them *oṉraiviṭṭa aṇṇaṉ* or *tambi* (r=ŋ).

Sagodari: sister, a learned word.

Akkā: elder sister. The eldest sister of the family is called *mūttakkā* or *periyakkā.*

Tañgacci: younger sister.

Tagappaṉ: own father; in address, *appu, aiya.* Now *pappa* and other foreign terms are used. *Tandai* also is used but is classical. *Pitā* is Sanskrit. The father's elder brother is *periyayyā* or *periyappu,* big father, which also designates the mother's eldest sister's husband. The father's younger brother and the mother's younger sister's husband are both *kuñciappu, ciṟṟappā,* that is, little father.

Tāy, own mother, corresponds to *tagappaṉ* and is the usual word; *aṉṉai* corresponds to *tandai, mātā* to *pitā.* The Tranquebar Dictionary gives *ammāḷ,* of which *amma* is the vocative. In Jaffina it is used only as an honorific term attached to a lady's name. The term of address is *ācci* or *ammā.* The mother's elder sister and father's elder brother's wife are called *periyammā* or *periyācci;* the mother's younger sister and father's younger brother's wife are called *kuñciyācci* or *kuñciyattai,* or simply *kuñci,* little.

Appā: father's father, mother's father.

Appācci: father's mother.

Pūṭṭaṉ: any great-grandfather.

Pūṭṭi: any great-grandmother.

Koppāṭṭaṉ: great-great-grandfather.

Koppāṭṭi: great-great-grandmother.

Kōnduru is the generation above *koppāṭṭaṉ,* and *mānduru* that above *kōnduru.*

Pētti or *pettācci:* mother's mother.

Magaṉ: son, man's brother's son, woman's sister's son, etc. *Tambi,* younger brother, also is used as a term of endearment for a son.

Magaḷ: daughter, man's brother's daughter, woman's sister's daughter. A man uses *tangacci,* younger sister, as term of endearment to his daughter.

Pēraṉ: grandson; addressed as *tambi,* younger brother.

Pētti means granddaughter, as well as mother's mother. She is addressed as *tangacci.*

Pūṭṭaṉ means great-grandson, as well as great-grandfather. Term of address: *tambi.*

Koppāṭṭaṉ: great-great-grandson.

B. CROSSED RELATIONSHIPS

I can find no term for this group as a whole.

Maccāṉ: father's sister's son, mother's brother's son, younger sister's husband, husband's brother, whether the brother is older or younger than the husband. The Tranquebar Dictionary gives *maccinaṉ.* It also gives *maittunaṉ,* which is from Sanskrit *maithuna,* paired, coupled, being a male and a female, connected by marriage. *Maccāṉ* is thus a Sanskritic word, and so is Sinhalese *massinā.*

Maccāḷ: father's sister's or mother's brother's daughter, brother's wife, husband's sister. The Sanskritic feminine *macciṉi* also occurs.

Māmā, ammāṉ: mother's brother, father's sister's husband. They can be distinguished as chief, great middle, little according to their place in the series of brothers. A "brother once removed" of the mother can be distinguished from her own brother as *oṉṟai viṭṭa ammāṉ,* "uncle once removed."

Māmi: father's sister, mother's brother's wife.

Marumagaṉ: man's sister's son, woman's brother's son, daughter's husband. *Marumagaḷ:* man's sister's daughter, woman's brother's daughter, son's wife. These two terms are translated in English works as "the other son," the "other daughter," and are adduced as evidence of a former matrilineal inheritance. But this translation ignores quantity and confounds two sounds which *we* spell alike, except for two dots, but which Tamil never confuses: ர , r, and ற , r̤. "Other" in Tamil is மாறு , *māru* (r = ŋ), not மரு , *maru.* Mr. Venacitamby suggests that this *maru* is the same as *maru,* marriage, and that *marumagan* is, therefore, a son by marriage.

A man commonly marries his *maccāḷ,* but there is a saying: "*Maccini illāviṭṭāl maccinipiḷḷai,*" that is, "If the cousin is not available, the cousin's daughter."

C. RELATIONSHIPS BY MARRIAGE

Purusaṉ, a Sanskrit word meaning male, man, translates as "our husband." In speaking of him the wife will say "they" (*avar*) or "my they" (*eṉṉuḍaiya avar*), or use the neuter plural *avai*. In calling him she will not use his name but will say "come hither," using a polite imperative: *iñjāruṅkaḷ,* or more colloquially *iñjāruṅko,* or simply *iñjārum.*

Peñcādi, the word for wife, is a hybrid from Tamil *peṇ,* female, and Sanskrit *jāti,* kind. Other terms are *maṉaivi* (from *maṉai,* house), *maṉair, maṉaiyāḷ, pāriyār* (Sanskrit), *illāḷ* (Tamil *il,* house), *pattiṉi* (Sanskrit). The last three terms are classical. The husband addresses his wife as *nīr,* you, the honorific plural, or *iñjārum,* come hither, polite, but less polite than when followed by *kaḷ* or *kō.* This same polite imperative is used for other relations, but then the term of relationship is used, as *māmi, ingē vāruṅkaḷ,* "aunt, come hither." If no term of relationship is used the wife knows she is being addressed.

Attāṉ: elder sister's husband.

The same system has been described by Rivers among the Todas. The language of this people being different, yet Dravidian, their kinship terms are different, yet similar. Rivers's phonetics are a bit doubtful. If Rivers is correct, the feminine is used for both male and female cross-cousin. Note that at least three of the terms given are Sanskritic. So much for the primitiveness of this people.

We have divided the Sinhalese and Tamil kinship systems into three groups, but the third group is very slight and rather artificial. There are indeed a few terms which are restricted to relations by marriage, but most of these relationships are expressed by terms belonging to the second group, crossed relationships. The reason is that as a man marries his cross-cousin his father-in-law is his uncle, his brother-in-law his cousin, and so on, all his relations by marriage being already related to him before marriage as crossed relations. In a consistent cross-cousin system, then, there should be no third group at all, and this is indeed the case in Fiji, where wife = female cousin, brother-in-law = cousin, and so on. The Tamil system comes near to that perfection, but the Sinhalese system is removed a little further from it by the use of in-law terms, all of which are Sanskritic in origin. We may, therefore, anticipate that this third group is due to the intrusion of Sanskritic terminology.

The influence of Sanskrit on the Tamil system is proved clearly by the presence of such Sanskritic words as *sagōdara, ayyā, maccāṉ,* etc. On the other hand, Tamil influence has certainly invaded Sinhalese kinship, as it has the Sinhalese language. Such words as *akkā, ammā,* cannot be traced to Sanskrit, but occur in Tamil, and therefore are doubtless Dravidian in origin.

III. Pali System

The expression *Pali system* is, in fact, inaccurate. Pali, as we have it, is merely a learned language used in their sacred writings by a variety of peoples who vary in their kinship systems. For instance, this language was used in Ceylon at a late period; but obviously the Sinhalese must have tended to use Pali kinship terms in a classificatory sense, whether this was or was not the usage of the people who first spoke the Pali language. Nevertheless, the original meaning must exercise a restraining influence on local usage, especially in the older words, and we shall, therefore, find it instructive to collect the Pali terms and note their use. I have had to work with the sole assistance of dictionaries, compiled by men unacquainted with kinship problems, and my own very limited acquaintance with Pali literature.

Mudaliyar A. Mendis Gunasekera has supplied me with mnemonic verses enumerating the "ten relationships," in Sinhalese *dasa näyo* (long *ä*):

Cūḷa mātā, cūḷa pitā, mahā mātā, mahā pitā,
Jeṭṭhabhātā, kaṇiṭṭhoca, tathā bhaginiyo duve,
mātulo, mātulānī ca dasa me ñātayo matā.

"The little mother, little father, great mother, great father, the elder brother and the younger, also both sisters, the maternal uncle and his wife, these are recorded as my ten relations."[5]

I do not know why these relations are selected: they are all collaterals, and cover only two generations.

Ñāti, the general term for a relation, comes from the root *jan, jñā,* to know. It is the same as Greek *gnotos*.

A. STRAIGHT RELATIONSHIPS

Bhātar: brother. In Jātaka No. 67 (Fausböll III, 306 ff.) it is definitely an own brother: the story would be pointless if it included father's brother's son. The story may not have originated in India, however, as it is the same argument by which Sophocles' Antigone justifies the sacrifice of a child to a brother. The term *sabhātar,* "own brother," is used in Mahāvaṁsa XLVIII 51 of a father's brother's son, but this passage is very late and so is no evidence for early Pali, but only for Ceylon custom.

Sodariya, literally "of the same womb," means an own brother in Jātaka I 308.

Jeṭṭha: literally "best," eldest brother.

Kaniṭṭha: youngest or younger brother. Another term is *anuja,* "born after."

It will be noticed that whereas Tamil and Sinhalese have no general term, except in learned language, for brother, but only terms for elder and younger brother, Pali does not really possess distinct terms for elder and younger brother: it simply adds the adjectives eldest and youngest to the word brother; the substantive is constantly dropped, so that *jeṭṭha* and *kaniṭṭha* come to be used as substantives equivalent to Tamil *aṇṇaṉ* and *tambi.* The history of these words shows clearly the interaction of two systems: one in which all brothers are designated by the same term, the other in which seniority is so paramount that there is no general term for brother, only one term for elder brother and one for younger brother.

Mātucchāputta, son of the mother's sister, occurs in Saṁyutta II 281. The word suggests that Pali had no term for the mother's sister's son or father's brother's son, what anthropologists call ortho-cousins. The presumption is that they were called brothers, but could be distinguished by a descriptive term like the present one from own brothers.

Bhaginī: sister. Dictionaries do not state whether it is used by women as well as by men. Its derivative *bhāgineyya,* to which we shall revert, suggests that it should properly be used only by a man to his sister, for *bhāgineyya* is always the father's sister's son, not the mother's sister's son.

Pitar: father. *Mahāpitar:* father's elder brother. *Cūlapitar* or *cullapitar:* father's younger brother.[6] *Pitar* is thus definitely used in a classificatory sense. *Pitar* is used improperly of the mother's brother in Mahāvaṁsa LXIII 53; it is a late passage, but if the writer followed Sinhalese usage he would not call this uncle father.

Petteyya, from *pitar,* is used of the father's brother in Mahāvaṁsa LXVI 8.

Mātar: mother. The expressions "great mother" and "little mother" are known to me only from the stanza quoted above.

Mātucchā, from Sanskrit *mātṛṣvasā,* means "mother's sister" (Vinaya II 256).

Ayyaka: grandfather. *Pitāmaha:* father's father. *Mātāmaha,* mother's father, is used in a classificatory sense in Jātaka IV 146. This passage is most important, as it is an ancient tradition which pictures a state of society that had come to an end, in Ceylon at least, before our records begin. There is every likelihood of its being a true picture of Sākyan society, a small but highly aristocratic principality which existed before the rise of the great kingdoms that wiped them out.

Mātāmahī: mother's mother.

Papitāmaha: great-grandfather, presumably paternal.

Payyaka: paternal great-grandfather.

Putta: son. In Mahāvaṁsa LXIII 51 it is applied to a sister's son. *Suta* also means son.

Dhītar: daughter. In the story of the Sākyas referred to above, the King of Kosala says, "Let them [the Sākyans] give me a daughter." This is not definite proof of a classificatory system, but it is exactly the way people with a classificatory system speak.

Nattar: grandson. In Mahāvaṁsa XXVII, 2, written in the fourth century A.D., it is used of a brother's descendant. *Paputta* also occurs.

B. CROSSED RELATIONS

Mātulaputta, mātulassa suto: descriptive terms for the mother's brother's son.

Pitucchāputta: father's sister's son.

Mātula: mother's brother.

Mātulānī: mother's brother's wife.

Pitucchā: father's sister.

Bhāgineyya: man's sister's son.

Bhaginīdhītar: man's sister's son.

C. RELATIONS BY MARRIAGE

Sāmin, sāmika, literally "lord, master": husband. *Bhattar* also is used.

Bhariyā, jāyā: wife. It seems to have been the custom, as in Ceylon, to call a mother "the mother of So-and-So," for the Buddha's wife is constantly called "the Mother of Rāhula." In fact, the author of the introduction to the Jātaka seems not to know her under any other name (I 58 et passim).

Devara: husband's brother. The Pali Text Society's Dictionary says the commentary on the Vimānavatthu explains it as "husband's younger brother." The Abhidānappadīpikā merely says "husband's brother." *Patibhātuka,* a descriptive term, occurs in Jātaka VI, 152.

Nanandar: husband's sister.

Sāla: wife's brother (known to me only in Abhidānappadīpikā).

Sasura: husband or wife's father. In early Pali, when the polite plural was not common, it is used to a father-in-law.[7]

Sassu: husband or wife's mother; also *sasurī.* A good woman treats her mother-in-law as a divinity.[8]

Sunisā, sunhā, husā: son's wife.

Jāmātar: daughter's husband.

Cross-cousin marriage occurs in the first part of the Mahāvaṁsa and in the early traditions it records. A man marries either his father's sister's daughter (VI, 20) or his mother's brother's daughter (IX, 16; X, 29 f.). The Buddha's genealogy shows cross-cousin marriage occurring with a regularity I have never seen among people where cross-cousin marriage is usual.[9] There is no reason to doubt the genuineness of this genealogy, and it may be taken to be good evidence of cross-cousin marriage among the Sākyas. Nevertheless, the Pali system is not a genuine cross-cousin system. In the first place it has no proper terms for crossed relationships, but only descriptive terms such as mother's brother's son, father's sister. Second, it has a complete set of terms for relations by marriage. Whereas in the Tamil and Sinhalese systems it was the distinction of the second and third groups that was forced, in Pali it is the separation of the first and second: it places the *pitucchā* in one category and the *mātucchā* in the other, although both terms are formed in the same way, the one from "father," the other from "mother," with the addition of "sister." It is difficult to resist the conclusion that a Sanskritic language was not the original language of the Sākyas, whatever it may have been in Buddha's time. The cross-cousin system, however, has had some influence on the Pali language: the term for uncle is not a descriptive term, but a derivative of *mātar,* and the nephew is designated by an adjective formed from the word for sister. The nephew seems to play an important part.

IV. Sanskrit System

The same remarks apply to the expression *Sanskrit system* as to the Pali system, but with less force. In its earliest form Sanskrit does more or less represent a people, and in its later stages it certainly went hand in hand with customs of which a good proportion was not Dravidian.

Relations on the father's side are called *jñāti*.

A. STRAIGHT RELATIONSHIPS

Bhrātar: brother. Böthlingk gives *pitṛvya putrabhrātaras,* "brothers who are sons of the father's brother." This proves the classificatory use of the word brother, but it also proves that the classificatory use was not normal; *bhrātar,* when alone, was understood to mean own brother. This is confirmed by the absence of *svabhrātar,* own brother; at least Böthlingk does not give it. In the *Rigveda* the term *bhrātar* is used of "deities who are brothers of one another or of the worshipper."[10]

Jyeṣṭha: eldest brother (R.V.).[11]

Kaniṣṭha, anuja: younger brother.

Svasar: sister (R.V.) *Kanīyasī:* younger sister.

Bhaginī, sister, is used in classical literature for a woman's sister (Manu II, 50). It is not clear whether this is the original use, or whether it was ever restricted to a man's sister. It appears only once in Vedic literature, and then much later in Nirukta III, 6. In the *Rigveda* we have *jāmī,* but authorities do not make it clear whether it is used only by men or also by women, or whether the text leaves this point doubtful. There clearly is no special term for an elder sister; she is called *jyāyasī svasar* (Manu II, 133).

Bhrātrīya: father's brother's son.

Mātṛṣvaseya and *mātṛṣvaseyi:* mother's sister's son and mother's sister's daughter.

Böthlingk defines *pitar* as "the father and his brothers." It seems to be used in a classificatory sense in Manu II.151. It certainly is so used much earlier in the Satapatha Brāhmaṇa XII.8.1.6. ff., for there are mentioned in succession *pitaraḥ, pitāmahaḥ, prapitāmahaḥ,* "fathers," "father's fathers," "great grandfathers" of an individual. Evidently "fathers" must here include "father's brothers."

Pitṛvya: father's brother.

Mātar: mother.

Matṛṣvasar: mother's sister. *Mātur bhaginī* occurs in Manu II 50.

Pitāmaha: father's father. It evidently is used in a classificatory sense in the passage of the Satapatha Brāhmaṇa referred to.

Pitāmahī: father's mother.

Mātāmaha: mother's father.

Mātāmahī: mother's mother.

Prapitāmaha: father's grandfather.

Prapitāmahī: father's grandmother.

Putra: son.

Duhitar: daughter.

Pautra: son's son.

Pautrī: son's daughter.

Napāt (*naptar*): in later literature this means the grandson; whether the son's son, or the daughter's son, or both, the dictionaries do not make clear. For the *Rigveda* Grassman's dictionary gives the following meanings: descendant, son, grandson. The dictionary and Prof. E. J. Rapson, who has kindly advised me, refer to VI.20.11, "thou didst return to the great father his own *napāt,*" and X.10.1, "the *napāt* of the father." Agni is at one time called the son of vigor (I.96.3), at another the *napāt* of vigor (II.6.2.). Prof. Rapson concludes that the original meaning was "descendant," and in later Sanskrit it was specialized as "grandson," in Latin as "nephew." We shall return to this point when dealing with the Roman system.

Naptī, Grassman says, means "daughter, granddaughter, the latter meaning however does not come out clearly."

Prapautra: son's son's son.

Prapautrī: son's son's daughter.

B. CROSSED RELATIONSHIPS

Relations on the mother's side are called *bandhu*.

Mātuleya: mother's brother's son. The feminine is *mātuleyī*.

Bhātṛvya is a kinship term of which the meaning is not certain. Delbrück explains it as meaning "a kind of brother," just as *pitṛvya* means "a kind of father," i.e., a father's brother. It is generally supposed to mean "mother's brother's son." I have shown in the *Indian Antiquary,* vol. LIV, 1925, p. 16, that this meaning agrees with the idea of rivalry that commonly attaches to the word.

Paitṛṣvaseyo bhrātar, maternal uncle's son, literally "brother" on the father's sister's side, occurs in the Mahābhārata and therefore after prolonged Dravidian contact. The adjective *paitṛṣvaseya* occurs alone in the same sense. *Paitṛṣvaseyī bhaginī,* "sister on the father's sister's side," is said to occur in Manu.

Māturbhrātra, literally mother's brother, is the old term for that kinsman, but later, in the Sūtra, *mātula* appears. Delbrück remarks that in the older Law Books where the *pitṛvya,* father's brother, and the *mātula* are mentioned, the father's brother takes precedence, and that the mother's brother distinctly comes to the fore in the Epics.[12]

Pitṛṣvasar: father's sister.

Bhāgineya: sister's son; apparently only a *man's* sister's son. *Svasrīya* also occurs, feminine *svasriya.*

C. RELATIONS BY MARRIAGE

The term *sambandhi* is used of relations by marriage.

Pati: husband. Atharvaveda XIV.2.1. may be using it of husband's brothers as well, for it says, "Mayest thou, O Agni, give to us husbands the wife." Satapatha Brāhmaṇa II.6.2.14 seems even more definite. There maidens walk round the altar and say, "As a gourd from its stem release me hence, not thence." The author adds, "When she says 'hence' she means 'from paternal relations' (*jñātibhyas*); when she says 'not thence' she means 'from the husbands' (*patibhyas*); for husbands are a support for the women."

Jāyā, bhāryā, patnī: wife.

Devar: husband's brother, more especially the younger one. In Vedic times he could take over the deceased brother's wife.

Svasurya: husband or wife's brother.

Nanandar (V): brother's wife.

Syāla (V): wife's brother. *Sakhī,* literally companion, also is used.

Jāmātar (V): sister's husband.

Svasura: father-in-law. This word apparently is used in a classificatory sense in Atharvaveda XIV.2.27: "Be pleasant to fathers-in-law." The daughter-in-law avoids her father-in-law, Atharvaveda V.8.6.24; Aitareya Brahmana III.22; Manu IX.62 (where the term for father-in-law is *guru,* venerable).

Svasrū (V): mother-in-law.

Duhitarpati: literally, "daughter's husband."

What is true of the Pali system applies with even greater force to the Sanskrit system. As we follow back the terms for crossed relations, even derivates like *mātula* disappear and only descriptive compounds like *mā-turbhrātra* occur. The further we ascend the less evidence we find of cross-cousinship. On the other hand, the classificatory use of certain terms is beyond doubt, and it only remains to be seen whether it occurs in other Indo-European languages.

V. Greek System

For this system I have drawn largely on Boisacq's *Dictionnaire étymologique de la langue grecque,* and on Liddel and Scott.

The general term for kinsmen is *étai.*

A. BLOOD RELATIONS

The Indo-European term for brother appears in Greek as *phrātēr, phrētēr,* but retains its original meaning only in Ionian. In other dialects it means "a member of a clan," *phrātría.* The term *adelphós* has supplanted *phrātēr* in the sense of brother; originally it was an adjective meaning "of the same womb," thus representing both in etymology and meaning the Sanskrit *sagarbha,* in meaning *sahodara.* The latter, as we have seen, still is used in Ceylon. This adjective qualified *phrātēr,* thus indicating brothers of the same womb, then *phrātēr* dropped out, leaving *adelphos* by itself to mean "own brother," while *phrātēr* alone meant a clan-brother. There can be no doubt then that *phrātēr* originally was classificatory and has remained so. Just as in Ceylon *sahodara* has succumbed to classificatory influence, so *adelphos* has been influenced so far as occasionally to mean any near kin. In the same way Homer uses *kasignētos* and *kasignētai* at times, it would seem, of cousins, though properly these terms refer to brothers and sisters by the same mother. In Sparta *káseis* were boys of the same class in gymnastic exercises. In Greece, however, the classificatory tendency was checked by the strong development of the individual system, whereas in Ceylon it was encouraged by Dravidian influence. The feminine of *adelphos* is *adelphē.*

Patēr: father. The plural also occurs in the sense of ancestors (Il. VI.209; Od. VIII.245).

Patruiós: stepfather, a late and rare term constructed on the analogy of *mētruia.* This is a new feature. There is no place for it in a classificatory system: there the stepfather usually is a man who was counted as a father before he married the mother.

Patrokasignētos, "father's brother," is a Homeric term. Later we find *patrádelphos* and *pátrōs,* which latter represents Sanskrit *patṛvya.* From the times of Euripides and Isaeus onwards we meet with *theîos,* uncle, father or mother's brother.

Mētēr: mother.

Mētruiá: stepmother.

Mētrōs: maternal uncle, Il. II.662; XVI.717.

Tēthís: father or mother's sister.

Delbrück says there is no term for a grandparent in Homer except *mētropátor,* mother's father, in Iliad XI.224. It must however be remembered that in metrical works the vocabulary is limited by the exigencies of meter; thus *mētropátōr* will fit into a hexameter, but not *mētromētōr,* mother's mother, which is possible in lyrics and therefore occurs in Pindar. That may be the only reason that Homer uses *mētros mētēr,* mother's mother (Od. XIX.416). *Patropatōr,* found in Pindar, would fit a hexameter, but *patromētōr,* a late term, would not. The metrical objection does not, however, apply to *páppos,* grandfather, the *tēthē,* later *mámmē,* grandmother. We must conclude that Homer did not use these terms because he did not know them, but knew only descriptive terms. Later writers adopted children's words.

Propatōr, "forefather," is used of the first founder of a family and of ancestors in general by Herodotos (II.161, 169; IX.122). *Prógonos* also occurs.

Paîs: child. In the law of inheritance, *anepsiōn paîdes* means descendants (Pauly-Wissowa, *Reallexikon,* s.v.).

Huiós: son.

Thugatēr: daughter.

Huiōnos, grandson, occurs in Iliad II.666, but Homer usually has *paidos pais,* child's child.

Anepsiós is the equivalent of Sanskrit *napāt.* In Herodotos it means both the father's sister's son and the father's brother's son (V.30; VII.82; IX.10). Herodotos also uses it of a man's sister's son (VII.5). In Herodotos V.30 we hear of an *anepsiós* who is also a son-in-law or brother-in-law (*gambrós*), a possible case of cross-cousin marriage.

Adelphidéos: a nephew, according to Liddel and Scott, but also sister's son, for instance Herodotos IV.147.

B. RELATIONS BY MARRIAGE

The general term in Homer is *pēós.* Later literature has *kēdestēs* from *kédos,* care, trouble, funeral rites; it may mean one for whom one cares, but it also may mean one for whom one has to celebrate funeral rites. It is, therefore, a word to keep in mind when discussing the religious side of kinship.

Gambrós also means one connected by marriage, but usually son-in-law. Homer also uses it for brother-in-law (Il. V.474), and the meaning father-in-law also is found.

Pentherós is the Sanskrit *bandhu,* relation on the mother's side, but it stands in Greek for any connection by marriage, more especially the father-in-law.

Daēr: husband's brother.

Gáloōs, gálōs: husband's sister.

Aélioi: men who have married sisters.

Hekurós: father-in-law. *Hekurá:* mother-in-law.

Núos: daughter-in-law, and hence a woman coming into the family; thus Aphrodite says she will not be an unfitting *núos* to Anchises' father, mother, and brothers.

Plato in his *Laws,* 926 A, speaks of marriage with a cousin as if it was the right thing. "It is possible that a nephew (*adelphidoús*), the son of a wealthy father, might not be willing to take his uncle's (*theîos*) daughter, because he is fastidious and has a view to a better match. It is possible also that he might be compelled to disobey the law owing to the lawgiver prescribing the greatest misfortunes by compelling him to ally himself with mad persons or to accept other misfortunes of body and soul, which to possess would make life not worth living." Unfortunately, the vagueness of Greek terms makes it impossible to be sure. If there was cross-cousin marriage in Greece it is not unlikely that traces will be found in the Balkans at the present day.

VI. Roman System

A. BLOOD RELATIONS

I have here used Pauly-Wissowa, Lewis and Short, and Walde's *Lateinisches Etymologisches Wörterbuch.*

Blood kinsmen as a whole are called *cognati.* The *cognati* include a smaller group of *agnati,* who are relations connected through persons of the male sex (*Gaius* III 10).

Frāter: brother. There was a college of priests called *frātrēs arvālēs.*

Soror: sister.

Delbrück quotes Digest XXXVIII. 10. fr. 10 15 on the use of *frater* and *soror. Quos quidam ita distinxerunt, ut eos quidem qui ex fratribus nati sunt fratres patrueles, item eas quae ex fratribus natae sunt sorores patrueles, ex fratre autem et sorore amitinos amitinas, eos vero et eas qui quaeve ex sororibus nati nataeve sunt consobrinos consobrinas quasi consororinos, sed plerique hos omnes consobrinos vocant.* "Some have distinguished them in the following way: they call those males who are born of brothers *fratres patrueles,* in the same way those females who are born of a brother and a sister *amitini, amitinae,* but those who are born of sisters *consobrini, consobrinae,* as it were 'connected through sisters' but many call these *consobrini.*" Thus *frater* and *soror* definitely were used by some authorities in a classificatory sense of children of two brothers, as opposed to children related through people of opposite sexes. They made the same distinction as is made in the cross-cousin system, but they added a further class which is unknown to, and inconsistent with, the cross-cousin system, namely the children of sisters. It looks as if this class was added to make the classification complete according to the notions of people unacquainted with the principles of the cross-cousin system.

Patruelis is derived from *patruus,* father's brother. It is commonly used alone to designate the father's brother's son. The process is exactly the reverse of that which took place with the Greek *phrāter adelphos:* in Latin it was the noun that took the restricted meaning and the adjective that preserved the classificatory sense. This different development lies in the meaning of the adjectives.

Amitinus, amitina, cross-cousin, and *consobrinus, consobrina,* mother's sister's son and daughter, also are properly adjectives. According to Walde, *amitinus* is formed from a familiar appellative *ama,* such as is common in most countries.

Pater: father; in the plural, forefathers, senators.

Mātēr: mother.

Patruus: father's brother. *Patruus magnus:* grandfather's brother. *Patruus major:* great-grandfather's brother.

Amita: father's sister.

Avunculus, literally "little grandfather," means "mother's brother."

Matertera: mother's sister.

Avus: grandfather: *proavus, abavus, atavus, tritavus.*

Fīlius: son.

Fīlia: daughter.

Nepōs: son's son, daughter's son; in post-Augustan, brother's or sister's son.

B. RELATIONS BY MARRIAGE

The general term is *affinis.*

Lēvir: husband's brother.

Glōs: husband's sister.

Socer: father-in-law.

Socrus: mother-in-law.

Gener: daughter's husband.

Nurus: son's wife.

When we pass to the systems of other members of the Indo-European group, even the scanty first-hand knowledge I have so far had at my disposal fails. I could do little more than repeat Delbrück, and must therefore refer to him. I shall content myself here with singling out those points that seem to have special bearing on the original nature of the Indo-European system.

VII. Persian System

Napā in old Persian means grandson.

Auis is the same word as Latin *avus,* but it means uncle (in our sense).

Herodotos gives a case in which a brother's daughter married a sister's son (VII. 82, with Stein's note, and genealogy at III. p. 24). One case is not enough, and I only mention it here in case more cases turn up.

VIII. Germanic System

Delbrück (p. 493; cp. 495) says that *oheim* is the mother's brother, sometimes the sister's son; that the word for mother's brother has been extended to the father's brother; that there is no Germanic word for brother's son. "One may well infer," he says, "that the paternal uncle addressed the children of his brother like his own, that is as son and daughter" (pp. 500, 502, 505).

Conclusions

The first conclusion that results from this review is that the Indo-European system was at some time classificatory. The indications were so clear that we need not recapitulate them.

It is almost equally obvious, however, that it had ceased to be truly classificatory before the splitting up of the various branches of this language. Terms like father, brother, and so on could still be used in a classificatory sense, but they usually referred to own father, own brother, etc., as in the modern systems. If they were meant in a classificatory sense it might be necessary to make this clear by the addition of some adjective such as "paternal." Unless we assume that the change from classificatory to individual had begun before the separation, it is difficult to explain how it comes that not a single of the derivatives remained out and out classificatory even in the earliest records we have of them, not even the Indian branch, which was in contact with classificatory systems and was influenced by them.

To what type of classificatory system did the Indo-European system belong? Certainly not the cross-cousin type. In India traces of the cross-cousin system disappear as we ascend to the earliest times. Such traces as we may find later must, therefore, be due to Dravidian influence. The history of the Tamil word *maccan* is instructive. If Sanskrit had had a word which meant cross-cousin and the Tamils wanted a Sanskrit word, they would have borrowed that word, but they borrowed a word which meant "connected by marriage"; we must conclude that this was the nearest equivalent to cross-cousin that the Tamils could find in Sanskrit. In the same way the Väddas use for cross-cousin a term which in Sanskrit means brother-in-law. I have emphasized the fact that Sanskrit has a set of terms for relations by marriage as well defined as the terms for crossed relationships are uncertain. The words for "in-laws" are remarkably constant in Indo-European languages, and this alone is sufficient evidence that the original system was not a cross-cousin one. Further, special terms for grandparents seem to form an organic part of a cross-cousin system. In fact, a perfect cross-cousin system seems to involve different terms for the father's father and the mother's father, since they belong to different groups, one being a straight relation, the other a crossed one; and the same applies to grandmother. But the Indo-European system seems to have lacked special terms for grandparents; they are merely fathers and mothers, or forefathers and foremothers, or best fathers, grandfathers, father's fathers, older fathers. Slavonic, Latin and Germanic are the only exceptions. The Slavs used a word which in other parts means uncle; the Latins used *avus,* of which the diminutive meant uncle; Icelandic used the same word as Latin, but the Persians used that word to mean uncle. Thus these three languages also had no proper term for grandfather, but used a word which also included the uncle. The same applies *mutatis mutandis* to the nephew and the grandson.

This confusion of grandfather and uncle, grandson and nephew, runs through the Indo-European systems, as will appear if we follow the fortunes of *avus* further. The old Bulgarian word means uncle; Gothic *awō* means grandmother; Old Icelandic *āe, afe,* grandfather; Old Irish *ave,* grandson.

Take the root *dhē:* Greek *theios* is the uncle on either side, Slavonic *dĕdu* is the grandfather, Lithuanian *dėdĕ* the uncle. Greek *tēthē,* grandmother, and *tēthís,* aunt, are at bottom the same. The root *nepotiya* shows the same confusion: Sanskrit *napāt* = descendant(?), grandson; old Persian *napa* = grandson; Greek *anepsios* = nephew, cousin; Latin *nepos* = grandson, but in post–Augustan it means nephew; old Lithuanian *nepotis* = nephew, grandson; old High German *nefo* = nephew, according to Delbrück the sister's son; middle Irish *niae* = sister's son.

We must, therefore, revise Prof. Rapson's opinion of *napāt.* It is evident that already in Indo-European times it had attached itself to two relationships in particular, grandson and nephew. If it was indeed used in Vedic of a son, it must have been by an extension of the meaning; such an extension would be the easier as son and grandson were not properly distinguished. There is a suggestion that *nepotia* was more particularly the man's sister's son and the daughter's son.

The use of the same term for both these relationships occurs elsewhere. For instance, in Fiji and Tonga the term *vasu* applies both to the man's sister's son and to the daughter's son. The former seems to be the proper meaning, but the *vasu* is considered to be *vasu* to the clan as a whole and not to the individual; he is thus *vasu* to his mother's "fathers," as well as her "brothers." Among certain tribes of Vanua Levu in Fiji, the mother's brother is called grandfather and the sister's son grandson. I do not mean to affirm any connection between this and the Indo-European usage. In Vanua Levu it seems to be correlated to another curious custom, by which a man calls his father's sister "elder sister" and is called by her "younger brother." Of this custom there is no trace in Indo-European languages. The resemblance may be accidental, but we must keep a mind open to the possibility that it is not accidental. We shall find it easier to do so if we abandon the theory that these kinship systems are the inevitable result of primitive gropings after organization, and if we look upon them as institutions which came into being in the same manner as our Parliament, our Church, our banking, and like them are liable to be copied or imitated.

The evidence we have reviewed suggests that the original Indo-European kinship system was something like this:

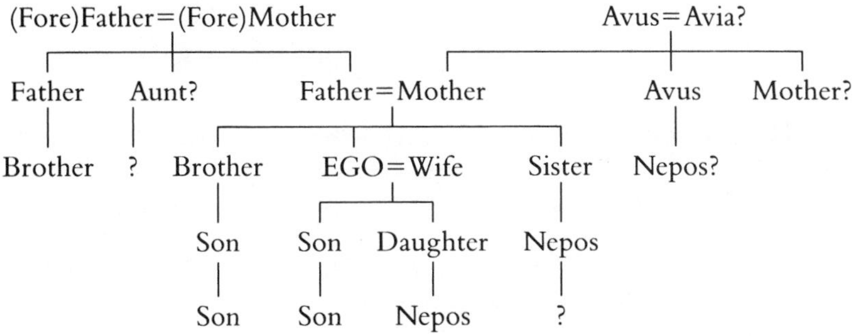

The relations by marriage are fairly straightforward.

Before closing the subject we cannot overlook the possible traces of a cross-cousin system that occurred in the course of our inquiry. There is the passage from Plato's *Laws;* the original use of the German *oheim;* the distinction made by some Roman authorities between *fratres patrueles* and *amitini;* the fact that the Sanskrit *bandhu,* a relation through the mother, is represented in Greek by *pentherós,* a relation by marriage. To these we might add the naming of a child after his grandfather in the modern Balkans.[13] I have been promised, but have never received, references to this custom in ancient Greece. We do not know for certain that this custom is an integral part of the cross-cousin system, but it constantly occurs in conjunction with it, and we might at least be prepared to find someday that it is the logical consequence of the system in its earliest form.[14] That earliest form may well be the alternate generation system, in which grandfather = grandson; that system appears in some obscure way to be connected with the cross-cousin system. A trace of the alternate generation system seems to be retained in Old Irish *aue,* which instead of meaning grandfather or uncle means grandson.

If that should happen, how are we going to explain these traces? There are two possible hypotheses. First, we may suppose that before being what we have supposed it to be the Indo-European system was a cross-cousin system, which disintegrated into a classificatory system of the type we have outlined. The other hypothesis is that the Indo-European system did not meet the cross-cousin system in India alone, but over the whole area from India to Ireland. It was only in India, however, that the cross-cousin system put up any real resistance and even regained some of the territory lost. Elsewhere it left only broken fragments and possibly some myths, such as the theft of ambrosia.[15] Personally, I incline to the latter hypothesis; but either of them has great possibilities, and whoever can decide the question finally will have written a most important chapter in the history of the development of European society.

Note on Indo-European Kinship

The previous article revised Delbrück's work on Indo-European kinship. Delbrück does not seem to have been acquainted with Tacitus' *Germania,* chap. XX, para. 4. "The sister's son is in as great honor with the uncle as with the father. Some consider this tie of blood more sacred and closer. . . . A man's heirs however and his successor are his children, and there is no will." (*Sororum filius idem apud avunculum qui apud patrem honor. Quidam sanctiorem artioremque hunc nexum sanguinis arbitrantur. . . . Heredes tamen successoresque sui cuique liberi, et nullum testamentum.*) Note the epithet *sacred.* Here, as elsewhere, the bond between maternal uncle and nephew is a religious one.

For naming after the grandfather in Greece we have such well-known cases as Kimon, son of Miltiades, son of Kimon: Xanthippus, son of Perikles, son of Xanthippus.

There is a suggestion of exogamy in *Dīgha* II 148: *Mallā ca, Mallaputā ca Mallasunisā ca Mallapajāpatiyo ca.* "The Mallas, sons of Mallas, daughters-in-law of Mallas, and wives of the Mallas." First we have

Ceylon Journal of Science, sec. G, vol. 2, pt. 1, 1928, pp. 33–4.

the heads of the families, their wives, their sons, their sons' wives: the daughters do not appear because they are married out, the sons-in-law because they belong elsewhere. The term Malla evidently refers to the chieftains, heads of families, as appears lower down on the same page, where each Malla is called forth in turn with his children, wife, *retainers* and *advisers*.

6

Buddha and Devadatta

Devadatta's constant, but unsuccessful, persecution of the Buddha, his cousin, is one of the main themes of Buddhist legend. It has usually been taken as a simple case of sectarian jealousy, requiring no further explanation. I believe there is a great deal more in it than that.

I will preface my remarks with the Buddha's genealogy. Spence Hardy, in his *Manual of Buddhism* (p. 140), relates how the thirty-two sons of Râma of the Kôli tribe married their thirty-two mother's brother's daughters of the Sâkya tribe. "From this time it became the custom of the Kôli and Sâkya tribes to intermarry with each other." This is borne out by the following pedigree taken from Rhys David's *Buddhism* and Spence Hardy:[1]

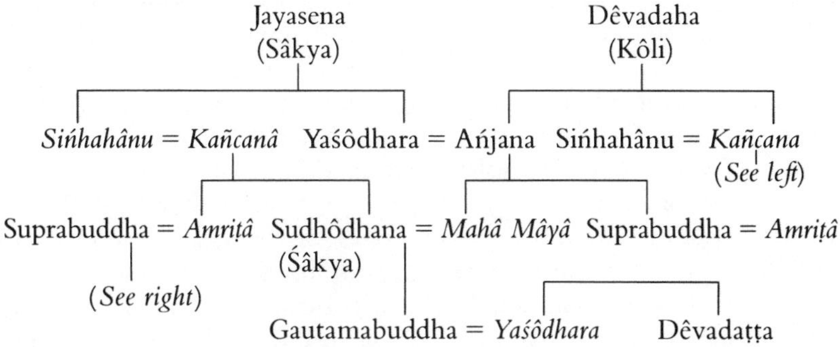

Indian Antiquary, vol. 52, 1923, pp. 267–72.

Anyone who has the slightest acquaintance with kinship systems will immediately diagnose the case. It is the cross-cousin system, under which a man's children are expected to marry his sister's children, but not his brother's children. In technical language, a man marries his cross-cousin, a term invented to express the fact that they are cousins through parents of opposite sexes. Such a form of marriage results in a system of reckoning kin in which the maternal uncle is the same as the father-in-law, the paternal aunt as the mother-in-law, and so forth, as anyone can work out for himself on the above pedigree.

This mode of reckoning kin is found in its typical form among the Tamils, the Tôdâs, and other peoples of South India,[2] among the Sinhalese ancient and modern, the Torres Straits Islanders,[3] the New Hebrideans, and in Fiji. With a trifling modification it occurs among the Seneca-Iroquois of North America.[4] Species of the same genus, or crosses between this and other species, are found broadcast from South Africa to America across the Pacific.

I assume straightaway that all these systems have a common origin. If we maintain that they have arisen independently, then good-bye to all history of civilization. We might just as well be consistent and say that the resemblances between Latin and Sanskrit or Malagasy and Hawaiian are accidental.

If all these systems have a common origin, we are justified in drawing inferences from one to another, provided we observe the laws of evidence. Just as we compare the Latin *pater* with the Sanskrit *pitar,* the Gothic *fadar,* and so hark back to an original *pater,* so we are justified in placing the Sakya custom beside the Sinhalese, the Fijian, and the New Hebridean, and thus restore the original practice from which all these varieties are derived.

In a series of papers I have described the beliefs and practices that center round cross-cousinship in Fîjî.[5] In Fîjî, groups intermarry just like the Kôli and the Śâkya, and this tribal relationship is variously described in different parts as *tauvu, veitambani, veimbatiki, veikila.* People who are so related make a point of abusing one another, calling each other "cad," "orphan," "body fit to cook"; they pull one another by the hair; they take each other's property without asking leave; on ceremonial occasions a man will seize a lot of stuff and get beaten in a playful way by his cross-cousins.[6] There is a great rivalry between such groups: "they are lands that vie with one another," says a Fijian; "it is a disgrace for them that the report should go forth that they have been overwhelmed in war, or in exchanges, or in eating, or in drinking."[7] All this rough handling, and rivalry, and abuse is done, mind you, in a friendly way; in fact, a man's proper "pal" is his cross-cousin, and tales are told of the endless tricks that inseparable cross-cousins played on one another. So essential is this cheating that over and over again tribes will derive their relationship from two gods of whom one cheated the other, who, thereupon, retaliated with bad language. So essential is the fighting that in the Windward Islands of Fîjî, where they have forgotten the meaning of *veitambani,* they will tell you that two tribes are *veitambani* because they could fight one another!

This constant feud between cross-cousins was not a local growth in Fîjî, for traces of it are found elsewhere. In the New Hebrides the two halves of society "are said to have different characters. . . . In the old time members of the two moieties hated one another and even now there is a feeling of enmity between the two."[8] Among the Thonga of South Africa, just as in Fîjî, the uterine nephew steals the offering and gets pelted by the others.[9] This, therefore, looks like an original feature of the cross-cousin system sufficiently ancient to have spread to South Africa at one end and to Fîjî at the other.

The reader will long ago have seen what we were coming to, namely to the conclusion that the rivalry between Buddha and Dêvadaṭṭa is an echo of the friendly and ceremonial antagonism of cross-cousins. We must leave it undecided, however, whether there existed between the Buddha and his cousin a friendly feud, which, with the disappearance of the custom, was misinterpreted as a bitter enmity, or whether in those days an originally friendly opposition had degenerated into hate, or whether, finally, there never was such a rivalry between the two, but traditions of cross-cousin rivalry became attached to the pair. It matters little to our purpose what may have been the case, for we are concerned here not with events but with customs, and it is sufficient if we can show that the legend of Buddha and Dêvadaṭṭa is evidence that similar customs once prevailed in Northern India as they do now in the Pacific.

At the suggestion of Rao Saheb S. Krishnaswami Aiyangar, let us consider the exact form taken by the feud between Buddha and Dêvadaṭṭa. "Shin-i-tian," quoted by Klaproth and Remusat in their edition of *Fa Hian* (p. 201), records a rivalry in mighty deeds between Naṇḍa, the Buddha's brother, and Dêvadaṭṭa, in which, of course, Naṇḍa surpasses his cousin. Late in life, according to Spence Hardy (*Manual of Buddhism,* p. 326), Dêvadaṭṭa thought thus: "I am equally honorable as to my family with Buddha; before I became a priest I was treated with all respect, but now I receive even less than my previous followers. I must take to myself 500 disciples; but before I can do this, I must persuade some king or other to take my part; great monarchs of Râjagaḥâ, and other places, are all on the side of Buddha; I cannot therefore deceive them, as they are wise. But there is Âjâsaṭ, the son of Biṁsâra; he is ignorant of causes, and disobedient to his parents; but he is liberal to his followers; so I must bring him over, and then I can easily procure a large retinue." Thus Dêvadaṭṭa enters into rivalry with the Buddha: the Buddha founds a monastic order, Dêvadaṭṭa must do the same; the Buddha is patronized by a great monarch, Dêvadaṭṭa must also seek such an exalted patron. Dêvadaṭṭa preaches "in imitation of Buddha" (p. 339); but, like our Fijian *veitambani,* Dêvadaṭṭa must go one better than the Buddha, only he does so in the spiritual, they in the material. When his Order falls to pieces he comes to the Buddha, and says (p. 337): "I have hitherto been refused that which I asked at your hands, but this is not right, as I am the nephew of Śudhôdana." (Here I must interrupt to inquire whether this is not an echo of the right a man's sister's son has of taking everything of his uncle's without his uncle being allowed to say him nay. Otherwise, what is the meaning of Dêvadaṭṭa's words?) Dêvadaṭṭa then proceeds to ask that on five points the discipline of the Order should be made more severe. The Buddha calls on men to leave the world and retire into monasteries; Dêvadaṭṭa wants them to retire to the forest. Buddha allows his disciplines to eat what is brought by the people to the monasteries; Dêvadaṭṭa wants them to eat nothing but what they have begged from door to door, and so on. The only motive that influences Dêvadaṭṭa from beginning to end is rivalry, a desire to surpass his cousin.

If the hostility of Dêvadaṭṭa is merely the record of ordinary hatred, it is difficult to understand why Dêvadaṭṭa possesses the power of flying through the air and of performing miracles (Spence Hardy, *Manual of Buddhism,* p. 326). Here we have a man who, according to existing accounts, is utterly wicked, so wicked as to oppose the Savior of the World, yet he is endowed with a power normally attained only after treading the path of meditation and renunciation towards the goal of sanctity. Buddhist tradition seems to have felt the difficulty, for it is at pains to explain that to him the power of passing through the air and of assuming any form was only a curse, which "led him on to do that which involved himself in ruin." If, on the other hand, this antagonism is really the echo or the continuation of an old sporting feud involving no moral stigma on either side, it is only natural that the rival chiefs should both be endowed with wondrous power; it is just that one surpasses the other. When at a later time it came to be interpreted as the malice of the Evil One against the Good One, a difficulty arose which had to be explained away. A similar difficulty beset our theologians of old, who accepted the wonders tradition ascribes to "Osiris, Isis, Horus and their train," yet, deeming them to be devils, were perplexed by the power wielded by the enemies of God, and were reduced to suppose that only

> Through God's high sufferance, for the trial of man,
> By falsities and lies the greatest part
> Of mankind they corrupted to forsake
> God their Creator.

But to return to our problem, can we find in modern India any evidence that the kinship customs were similar to those that now prevail in Fîjî, any trace of that playful antagonism of cross-cousins? Unfortunately, kinship and its customs have not received the attention they deserve, and so there is a dearth of evidence. I have made inquiries in Ceylon and this is the result: "If cross-cousins are of equal age they talk to one another like chums. If they are of different ages the younger one treats the older as if he were his elder brother. Brothers don't discuss private matters, such as love affairs, with each other, but cousins of equal age discuss such matters freely. They call each other names, if they are angry. . . . Brothers abuse one another when they are very young." All that survives in Ceylon is a greater familiarity between cross-cousins, and even that is restricted by the respect for age, which is such that "a man will address his servant as *ayya* (elder brother), if he is older."

Thanks to Rao Saheb S. Krishnaswami Aiyangar, I am able to produce more definite evidence from South India. I will quote his letter: "Whether they actually marry or no, these cross-cousins usually enjoy that license, particularly as between men, to indulge in free talk, which between others would be regarded as insulting. As between these cousins there is infinitely more freedom of talk. This habit has even invaded the castes to whom marriage between cross-cousins is a prohibition, such as, for instance, the Brâhmans. The habit is almost general among all classes other than that of the Brâhmans."

Another way of approaching the problem is by looking for divisions that fight one another. The only case I know of is the hostility between the right-hand and left-hand factions of Southern India, as described by Dubois in his *Hindu Manners and Customs* (Oxford ed., p. 25). The left-hand includes the Vaiśyas, a high caste, and also the lowest of all. The right-hand consists of most of the higher Śûdras and of the Parias. Their disputes center, it should be noted, round religious ceremonies. It may be objected that these two groups do not intermarry and that there is no evidence that they ever did; on the other hand, there is no evidence that they did not. The rigidity of caste admittedly is not early. Even at the present day cases of intermarriage are not uncommon, and I need not dwell upon them beyond quoting Mr. H. Codrington's information as regards Ceylon: "The castes used to intermarry, i.e., a higher-caste man took a wife from the caste next below. This is still done in parts of Ceylon by the Hali (*Salagama;* Tamil, *Śâliyar*) and Vahunpurayo."

But whether castes ever intermarried or not, the Tamil and Sinhalese kinship system is there to prove that there must at one time have been in the South intermarrying groups like the Sakya and Kôli, for the Tamil system is based on the dual organization and is sufficient evidence of its former existence. If in Tamil land this system divided the clans into two intermarrying groups, we should get back to a state of society such as exists in Fîjî. There each state is divided into two groups of clans: the nobles and their councillors or heralds are always in one,[10] the vanguard in the other. It can be shown that marriage into the other half was, until recently, the proper thing, but the nobles have tended to form alliances with the nobles of foreign states and thus to become endogamous within their rank or caste; the carpenters are strictly endogamous because no one will marry into them, they are so despised.

The Tôdâs, who have the cross-cousin system, are divided into Tartharol and Teivaliol. These two divisions do not now intermarry, but the following custom is significant. When a girl reaches a certain age "a man belonging to the Tartharol, if the girl is a Teivali, and to Teivaliol, if she is a Tarthar, comes in the daytime to the village of the girl, and, lying down beside her, puts his mantle over her so that it covers both and remains there for a few minutes. Fifteen days later she is deflowered by a man of either division."[11] This looks very much like a survival of the time when a woman's proper husband came from the opposite division. She still, in the majority of cases, finds her official paramour in the opposite division.[12] The Tôdâs therefore constitute the first link in the chain with which we want to connect the Tamil social organization with the Fijian. Students of Indian society may well find some more links among the backward tribes of India, for those who are out of the swim of civilization move more slowly and often are to be found now exactly where their neighbors stood thousands of years ago.

The use of the terms *right* and *left*, as applied to social divisions, lends probability to my suggestion. Among the Elema of New Guinea the clubs are divided into right and left. If I understand Dr. Seligman's note, the right and left intermarry, but not right with right, nor left with left.[13] The Galla of East Africa also divide society into a right and left wing, each of which can only marry into the other.[14]

I must apologize for producing such flimsy supports to the argument. As a matter of fact, they are intended not as proofs, but as clues for dwellers in India and round the Indian Ocean to follow up, and thus link up Africa and the Pacific with Northern India. Such a result might have far-reaching consequences, so far-reaching that I am almost afraid of hinting at them for fear of being utterly discredited, but here goes.

The antagonism of the Buddha and Dêvadaṭṭa is that of Good and Evil, which appear again in the persons of Osiris and Seth, Aḥura Mâẓda and Angro-Minyus, Christ and Satan, the Dêvas and Aṣurâs. If it is based on the rivalry of two intermarrying groups, may not those other antagonisms go back to the same source? In Fîjî we have seen that the gods of intermarrying tribes overreach one another just as their descendants do. May not the same have happened in other parts of the world, and the rivalry of the tribesmen be shared by their gods? I must insist that this institution is essentially religious: in Fîjî the relation of *tauvu* is defined as "having gods in common," and a man who resents the seizing of property by his cross-cousins is made ill by the spirits. In South Africa the pelting of the uterine nephew is part of a religious ceremonial. The story of the malice of Dêvadaṭṭa has only been preserved by the Buddhist religion. It is not surprising, therefore, that a feud which is essentially religious should have been preserved in the annals of religion, nor that, once the custom had died out, the tradition should have been misunderstood and an animus crept in which was not there before. Scholars may fail to see how a theory of good and evil can have arisen out of a mere system of intermarriage, but it is not a mere system of intermarriage; it is an elaborate theology, of which the intermarriage of two tribes or families is only one consequence. That theology is only beginning to unfold itself. As the picture becomes clearer and more detailed we shall cease to find it difficult to believe that the powers of good and evil go back to the ceremonial antagonism of intermarrying groups.

Appendix A

I should like to draw the reader's attention to *Vinaya,* vol. II, p. 188, where Dêvadaṭṭa approaches Buddha most respectfully and offers to relieve his age of the burden of administering the Order. The Buddha replies with abuse, calling him "corpse, lick-spittle" (*chavassa, kheḷâkapassa*). This seems scarcely in keeping with the character of the Buddha, but it is in keeping with that of a cross-cousin.

Dêvadaṭṭa is hurt, and one day when Buddha is walking up and down on Gṛdhrakûṭa hill throws a stone at him (*op. cit.*, p. 193). Hiuen Tsiang saw the stone, which was 14 or 15 feet high.[15] Evidently, we have here an old world legend of a type that covers a good part of the world, and is far more ancient than Buddhism. An example from the Pacific will be found in my "Cult of the Dead in Eddystone Island," pt. II.[16] It is remarkable that in Fîjî this kind of legend is often told to account for the cross-cousinship. Thus the people of the island of Nayau and of Vanuavatu intermarry a great deal and are relations (*veiwekani*); they tell a legend which is the nearest approach I can think of to the legend of Gṛdhrakûṭa. The gist of it is that the ancestor god of Nayau stole the water which the ancestor god of Vanuavatu had hung on a tree while he was at work. When the god of Vanuavatu discovered this he looked towards Nayau and saw the god of Nayau fleeing towards Nayau. He picked up a stone and threw it, and struck the bottles so that they broke. The stone broke in two and one half is in Nayau.

A similar legend, without the stone-throwing, is told to explain why Undu in Totoya and Natokalau in Matuku are tribal cross-cousins (*lauvû*).

Appendix B

Rao Saheb S. Krishnaswami Aiyangar has given me further particulars about the abuse usual among cross-cousins, from which it appears that they indulge in obscenities: "These expressions have reference more or less to matters of banter not usually permissible except as between husband and wife." Among the hill tribes of Fîjî the banter of cross-cousins alludes to sex.[17]

I think enough has been said to show that the use of abusive language among cross-cousins is a very ancient feature of the cross-cousin system, as ancient as the nearest common ancestor of the people who introduced the system into India, the New Hebrides, and Fîjî. It follows that normally Siddartha and Dêvadaṭṭa would have behaved in this characteristic manner.

7

The Basis of Caste

So much has been written about caste without bringing about a decision in favor of any particular theory that the public is perhaps a little weary of the discussion. Yet the late M. Senart's admirable reasoning[1] has shown that definite progress can be made. He has, I think, achieved a positive result in disposing of two theories, the occupational and the racial, which are derived rather from preconceived notions about primitive society than from the facts they profess to explain, and least of all from the point of view of the people who have developed the system and work it at the present day, and who are therefore our best guides. The occupational theory, for instance, seizing upon the obvious fact that caste and profession or trade are closely connected, hastily concludes that caste is based solely on a man's occupation and is the inevitable result of specialization in arts and crafts. If it had gone a little deeper it would have found that caste and craft are by no means as identical as is commonly supposed in Europe. Since this idea that an Indian is predestined to his craft by heredity is one of the main obstacles in the way of understanding the caste system, we may be excused for dwelling on this point even after M. Senart's cogent little treatise.

It is not the case that an Indian has no choice of occupation, but must

Acta Orientalia, vol. 14, 1935, pp. 203–23; reprinted, with minor alterations, in A. M. Hocart, *Caste* (London: Methuen, 1950), pp. 1–23.

follow that of his father, that he must shave or cook or fish as his father did. I have had to explain to tourists laboring under that misconception that my cooly gang, for instance, included anything from farmers, who probably had never handled a plough or sown a seed, down to drummers who may not know one end of the drum from the other, and cobblers who had never stitched a shoe; that the bar and commerce of Ceylon are largely in the hands of fishermen who would scorn to fish; that my food has been cooked by a farmer, by one who styles himself a merchant, but never, to my knowledge, by a member of the cook caste. Not all washermen wash, nor because you see a person washing are you safe in concluding that he is a washerman by caste. The state of affairs in Ceylon is this: a man may wash his own clothes; the mother, the elder sister, anyone in the family may wash the clothes, "but," says my informant, "we do not take outside washing; it would be a disgrace to the caste." If clothes are given out to be washed, as is usual, they will be given to a washerman, if one is available; otherwise to a man of some other low caste. Not every man who drums is a drummer: in Ceylon you often can see women of good caste sitting round a big drum,[2] and whiling away the idleness of a festive day with varying rhythms; but neither their sex nor their caste would officiate as public drummers at a temple, a wedding, or a funeral. Farming is the vocation of the highest caste in Ceylon, yet washermen so habitually till the fields that they have special field superintendents who are distinguished by a different title from the field superintendents of the farmer folk.[3] This latitude is not modern, not brought about by the disturbing influence of European example, for Manu allows the priestly caste to live by agriculture and trade, a permission of which Brahmans in South India avail themselves.[4] The royal state was the prerogative of the royal or noble caste;[5] yet in ancient days low caste men, washermen and others, not uncommonly became kings.[6]

Evidently, the common European notion that caste is hereditary handicraft does not tally with the facts. We must conclude that it derives from some other principle. We must search for that principle not in our minds, but in the minds of those people who practice the caste system, who have daily experience of it, and are thus most likely to have a feeling for what is essential in it.

If I go to seek for it among the Sinhalese and the Ceylon Tamils it is for the simple reason that it is the only part of the Indian world where I have experience of caste as a living organism. Apart from that it is not a bad area to seek in; Ceylon, despite its roads, estates, Colombo, and a swarm of officials, still remains very archaic in some respects. One still gets some of the atmosphere of the Jatakas, that is, of a very ancient India, long before the advent of Mohammedanism. The sequel will demonstrate this to some extent.

II

Before we can ask the people themselves, with any hope of understanding them, what is their idea of caste, we must have some acquaintance with the facts of the system, for they will inevitably assume some such knowledge, and if we have not got it we shall be talking at cross purposes. I will, therefore, give a very brief outline of the hierarchy as it exists in Ceylon.

The first caste among the Sinhalese once was the royal one, but it is now extinct. The former existence of the brahmanic or priestly caste is attested by ancient writings and by such place names as "brahman village." The disappearance of these two castes leaves the first rank to the farmers. They must once have shared equal honors with the merchants, a caste the former existence of which can be inferred from village names and the names of ancient streets.[7] Curiously enough, this farmer aristocracy forms the vast majority of the population of the old Kandyan kingdom. On the coast their predominance is much reduced by the presence in great force of fishermen.

The members of the three leading castes, extinct or surviving, are known as the "good people." They are opposed to the "low castes," which comprise fishermen, smiths, washermen to the "good people," tailors, potters, weavers, cooks, lime-burners, grass-cutters, drummers, charcoal burners, washermen to the low castes, mat-makers, and, most despised of all, the Rodiyas, shunned by everyone.[8] These castes often are subdivided: there are different ranks of farmers, and the fishermen are divided according as they fish with nets, rods, boats, and so on; the *vahunpura* and the *durāva* are said to be an upper and a lower division of the same caste.

The Tamils of the North of Ceylon have much the same castes: the kings are extinct, the brahmans and merchants imported, so that the farmers again are the highest indigenous caste; then come the low castes.

Manu also contrasts the "good people" with the lowest.[9] The division can be traced to the earliest literature, in which the aristocracy are called *ārya,* that is "worthy," "noble," as opposed to *śūdra,* a term of uncertain origin which may be translated as *serf.* The aristocracy was distinguished by wearing a sacred thread over the left shoulder, and was subdivided into kings, priests, and farmers. The first two, again, form an aristocracy within the aristocracy.[10] It has been much debated whether the farmers of Ceylon are the lineal descendants of the original farmer caste, the *vaiśya,* or whether they are a low caste that now finds itself at the head of society owing to the demise of the upper three. Since the Tamil farmers used to admit that they were *śūdra* and do not wear the sacred thread, the second view seems to be the right one. But this discussion is of no interest for us: this is not a legal argument. We are no more concerned with the question of whether the Ceylon farmers are heirs of the body of the ancient farmers than the student of the institution of monarchy is concerned with the legitimacy of the House of Hanover. All we need trouble about is whether the Ceylon farmers occupy the place and perform the functions of the old farmer caste. This they undoubtedly do, holding such ranks as village headman and all the offices of state other than the priestly ones, feeding the king and temple, and receiving service from the lower castes. Modern Sinhalese society thus differs from the ancient one only in so far as the aristocracy is single and no longer threefold.

In addition to the four castes, Buddhist writings occasionally mention a fifth, which in one place is called "the low one," as opposed to the exalted one of the kings and priests. This low caste is composed of five divisions: *caṇḍāla,* bamboo-workers, hunters, chariot-makers, and scavengers. Manu, on the other hand, declares that there is no fifth caste, and it is evident that the term is applied to this group loosely: they form no part of the four caste system, but lie outside it. There is no general term for them, so that Buddhist writings must refer to them by the name of the first division or a compound of the first and last. They are not allowed to dwell in the city or the village, whereas the serfs or artisans have a definite quarter assigned to them. Manu will not allow them a permanent residence at all, and they are called "known by day" because they may not appear in public except in the daytime.[11] In short, they lie outside the pale of society with its fourfold division, and they are rightly described by Europeans as outcastes. I am not aware that at the present time any distinction is made in Ceylon between low castes and people outside the caste system, or outcastes. Yet, if the term does not exist, the institution does: the Rodiyas are completely outside the pale; they do not, like the barbers, drummers, and the rest, form a necessary part of the social system, fulfilling certain indispensable functions; they are completely excluded. "They are," says Knox, "to this day so detestable to the People, that they are not permitted to fetch water out of their Wells; but do take their water out of Holes or Rivers. Neither will any touch them lest they should be defiled . . . They do beg for their living; and that with so much importunity, as if they had a Patent for it from the King, and will not be denied."

We need not insist on the restrictions to which the intercourse between one caste and another is subject, since it is the aspect that has most struck outside observers and is almost the best known. Thus, in the North Central Provinces of Ceylon the farmers will not intermarry with the drummers, nor eat with them, nor even accept a drink of water from them. They will, on the other hand, eat with the Vanni caste out of the same plate, but the two will not intermarry or attend each other's funerals. There is a case of one-sided intermarriage: the higher will marry women of the lower, but not vice-versa.[12] These are but commonplace instances. The reader who wishes to follow the fantastic variety of these regulations can do so in the second chapter of the third part of Knox's *Ceylon* and in the fourth chapter of M. Senart's book, while we pass on to inquire what it is that the people who actually work the system regard as most fundamental in it.

III

Let us ask them. To the question "What is caste?" a Tamil friend answers: "The castes have a particular work to do for the cultivator. This is how it is generally understood." Another Tamil, giving evidence before a commission, states that the low castes "were only service classes, such as washermen and barbers. Such low caste people in olden days were treated by their masters as their own children." A third Tamil gentleman writes: "One thing that ought to be borne in mind is that the Tamil chieftain lived as a feudal lord with all his vassals round about him. He had therefore slaves and vassals to serve him on all occasions, and these slaves and vassals represented different castes who served him in such capacity whenever occasion demanded. The vassals were called *kuḍimai* and the slaves *aḍimai*." I will add that *kuḍimai* is from *kuḍi,* a house. By vassals, therefore, my informant means household retainers.

The point of view of rude Sinhalese villagers lost in the jungle of the North Central Province is the same, only they cannot define, they can only illustrate. The farmers of one village make the following statement: "The people of Kadurupiṭiya are drummers . . . They are like servants: when called they must come for dancing, festivals, processions. The farmers give the drummers food on a leaf, also cash for their hard work. When the drummers come for a propitiation ceremony they are given clothes; only then."

Thus, what is uppermost in the minds of all our witnesses is the idea of service: the farmers are feudal lords to whom the others owe certain services, each according to his caste. But what kind of service? To the European the drummers are just men who make a noise on a drum; to a native they are much more than that. This is clearly shown in the polite title by which our farmers referred to the drummers: they did not call them "drummers," as I have rendered it, but "astrologers."[13] For them, clearly, drumming is not the essence of the calling, but only one manifestation of that essence, the other manifestations being dancing and ceremonies known as *bali.* In Sinhalese *bali* means an offering of food to various beings, and in Pali an offering to subordinate deities and to demons;[14] but in Ceylon it has connected itself more particularly with planets: if a man is afflicted by a planet, they make a statue of the planet, tie a string to one end and give the other end to the patient; then with appropriate ceremonies the astrologer-drummers rid him of his disease.

Drummers specialize in two directions: there are those who beat the demon drum, and those who beat the temple drum.[15] The demon drummers carry out ceremonies to expel demons; for instance, there is the *tovil* to cure diseases caused by demons,[16] in the course of which the drummers, wearing demon masks, dance and make offerings[17] of the blood of fowls and other animals; the demons are afraid and depart. We now seem to have got at the principle from which the various activities of the drummer are derived: he is primarily a demon-priest, and it is as such that he dances and drums. He identifies himself with his spirits by wearing a mask. This may explain why "the good people" will not beat a drum ceremonially, but have no objection to doing so in play, and why it is the work of "the good people" to put on masks and dance at processions—because "they do it in play"—but they would not for the world wear masks and dance in a demon ceremony. The drummer is the priest of an inferior cult, which the good people use although they do not perform, just as with us respectable people may consult a fortune teller but would scorn to be one. To supplicate the demon is one thing, to impersonate him quite another. A respectable person must fear demons because they are connected with death, but for that very reason he must not be identified with them. The connection of demons and planets, and so of drummers, with death is clearly expressed in a Sinhalese poem entitled "Demon-dancing." "The principal thing for this country and for the Sinhalese is the worship of planets. This custom prevails in the world and is appointed to mankind as a painful duty. The representation of the planets *in the burying place* has been made from the beginning."[18]

This view of drummers is confirmed by the distinction the Tamils of Ceylon draw between musicians and drummers. The musicians officiate at temples and on auspicious occasions, such as weddings, ear-borings, and house-warmings, and they rank about fifth among castes, that is, fairly high in the scale. The drummers, familiar to us all under the name of Pariahs, officiate at funerals and sometimes at temples when sacrificial victims are slaughtered, such a blood-stained worship being considered low. These drummers come last but one.

In conclusion, the drummers are a kind of priests, and that is why they form a caste, for priesthood is hereditary in all but a few advanced cults. They are a low caste because their cult is low, albeit necessary. Let us now see how far these conclusions explain other castes.

To the European the barber is just a man who shaves others, the washerman a man who does the laundry. For a native these two mean much more than that. "Practically on every occasion," says my first Tamil witness, "the barber and the washerman will have to be present. They are called the children of the family."[19] When we analyze what he means by "occasions" we find that he has in mind festivals, such as weddings, funerals, etc. Thus, at a Tamil wedding the musicians[20] walk before the bridegroom, the washerman spreads cloths for the bridegroom (who for the time being is the god Śiva) to walk upon. "In the rear other washermen, assisted by barbers, sing or howl [*sic*] blessings and praises of which he [the bridegroom] is the subject."[21] The barber carries the *tal,* or marriage necklace (the equivalent of our marriage ring), and the cloth called *kuṛai* for the bride. What the bridegroom wears while he is being shaved becomes the perquisite of the washerman and the barber. At a funeral the barber, the washerman, and the drummer are sent for, not the musicians. Men of the domestic servant caste (*koviyar*) carry the body to the cremation ground. "The barber prepares the fire for the cremation, and conducts the person who lights the fire three times round the pyre." "On the completion of each circuit he knocks a hole in the pot" which he holds.[22] In the words of one of my informants, "He is like a priest on the cremation ground. The priest who conducts ceremonies in the house does not go to the cremation ground . . . When the fire is burning the barber takes one or two pieces of bone and keeps them till the thirty-first day ceremony . . . After pouring water to extinguish the fire he ploughs the land and sows gingelly and eight kinds of grain." In Travancore the barber has a Sanskrit title which means "one who helps souls, indicating their priestly functions in the ceremonial of various castes."[23] Evidently, that is what looms large in the minds of the people, not shaving, which is merely one item in his priestly functions. I shall give another illustration of these from a Bant funeral in Southern India: at the end of it "a washerman touches those who attend with a cloth, and a barber sprinkles water over them. In this manner they are freed from pollution."[24] There are times when a brahman sprinkles water, but not on the cremation ground.

In the words "*he is like a priest on the cremation ground*" we have the key to the whole problem. The barber and the washerman, like the drummers, are not so much technicians as priests of a low grade, performing rites which the high caste priest will not touch. The brahman, priest of the immortal gods, can have nothing to do with death. For funeral rites the Tamils of Ceylon have to call in a man of the Śūdra caste who does not eat meat and who is termed a "Śiva teacher";[25] but even he cannot approach the extreme pollution of the cremation ground, so at this point the barber and the washerman have to take over from him. Because of the pollution involved the two are low caste.

The barber may be low, but there are lower than he whom he will not shave and who must, therefore, have barbers of their own. That is the case of the Chaliyan weavers; note that their barbers are also their chaplains.[26]

I had for some time been suspecting that the low rank of the washerman had something to do also with the washing away of the menstrual blood, when Mr. M. M. Wedderburn independently put forward the same view, and supported it with the following incident. A Sinhalese police inspector belonging to the washerman caste was sent to investigate a murder. He came to search the suspected house for traces of blood. This annoyed a woman of the house, who was of better caste. She threw at his head a lot of cloth stained with menstrual blood, saying, "There, washerman, are your blood-stained clothes." After all, the close association is loudly proclaimed in one of the titles by which the washerman is known. He is addressed as *koṭahaluvā,* "he of the short-cloth"; now the short-cloth feast is the feast held at the first menses of a girl when he brings clean clothes and receives as gift those she wore.[27] He also deals with the pollution of birth, or rather his wife does, for no servant, not even the nurse, will have anything to do with the soiled sheets, but Mrs. Washerman is notified and comes to remove them.

In Ceylon the washerman, like the drummer, appears in demon-worship. According to Parker, the two assistants of the demon priest who dances the dance of the Sinhalese God of the Rock are the washerman who washes his clothes and the smith who made the god's emblem.[28]

This, incidentally, brings out the connection of the smiths with the ritual: they make emblems, statues of the gods, temple jewelry. They work also for the family rites by making wedding necklaces, for instance. It is indeed possible that all jewelry began as ritual accessories.

In South India, potters sometimes officiate as priests[29] in temples of village goddesses[30] and of the god Aiyanar. They used to make sepulchral urns. Painted hollow clay images are made by special families of potters known as priests, who, for the privilege of making them, have to pay an annual fee to the headman; he spends it on a festival at the caste temple. They make images of the seven virgins for childless couples, ex-votos, horses on which Aiyanar rides down demons. The potters provide the pots which represent the gods at weddings. Even the making of pots for domestic usages has a ritual element, for the potter never begins his day's work at the wheel without forming into a phallus and saluting the revolving lump of clay, which, with the wheel, resembles the symbols of Śiva in the temples. In fine, the potter too is a kind of priest, and we need not be surprised when he claims to be of priestly origin, to be descended from Kulālan, the son of Brahmā. He prayed to Brahmā to be allowed, like him, to create and destroy things daily; so Brahmā made him a potter.[31] In Ceylon, I was told, they wear the sacred thread peculiar to the well-born castes "because they claim to be Brahmans: as Brahmā fashioned men, so they fashion pots, images without breath." The potters can quote in their support Buddhist traditions of a pot-making god Brahmā who was a potter in a former existence, and later became the great priestly god.[32]

If we believe the potters, as everyone seems to do in India, we shall be in a position to understand one of their functions which at first sight seems to have no connection with pot-making: they deal with dislocated bones and all kinds of fractures, leaving boils, wounds, and tumors to the barbers. Now the priests of Vedic times periodically created the world, not indeed its matter, but its essence or force, by fashioning a clay pan which was made equivalent to the world by carefully designed rites and words of power.[33] Things can be renovated, mended, by acting upon clay images of them, so pot-making and bone-setting go together. Then why should the potter be of inferior status to the brahman? In the words "images without breath" I think we hold the clue. The brahman puts breath, life, into the idol at the ceremony of its consecration, or putting in of the eyes;[34] the potter cannot. He has specialized in the manual side of this operation; he continues to make images and mend men with his hands, while the scholarly brahman continues to mend things by means of the Word. In a country where learning is as arrogant as it is in India, it is not surprising that the potters have sunk while the scholars have soared.

I could go on to show how the carpenters make the temple car in return for grants of land, how Billava toddy-drawers of South Canara officiate as priests at devil shrines, and so go on piling instances on instances,[35] but science does not consist in piling up instances; rather, it consists in finding the principles underlying a set of facts. Once this has been ascertained beyond doubt there is no more point in collecting more illustrations of a custom than there would be in studying the fall of every apple after the law of gravitation has been established. What we want is not quantity, but quality: a few decisive facts are worth tons of indecisive. Can anything be more decisive than the case of the Sinhalese caste known as jaggery men, but more aptly described as cooks?[36] Food in ordinary life is prepared by the housewife or the servants of whatever caste. At the Temple of the Tooth the cook is a farmer, not a jaggery man. Then where does the cook caste come in? Ask a Sinhalese: he will tell you they come to farmers' weddings and other festivals to cook. The scullion at the Temple of the Tooth is of the cook caste, but so are the night-watchers, who have nothing to do with cooking. Evidently cooking is not the essence of their calling, but menial service in ceremonies and temples, including kitchen work.[37]

As a last illustration we may take the *durayā,* or "servant caste," of Ceylon. They are split up into three divisions:[38] the first keeps watch, makes triumphal arches, sweeps, and so forth, at the eight great Buddhist sanctuaries of Anuradhapura; the second performs the same services at the Temple of the Tooth; the third lives by doing hired work. Thus the first two are based on temple service; as for the third, it is not clear, for the occasions on which such people are called in are not stated in my information.

We may wind up the argument by pointing out that in India every occupation is a priesthood; for the idea that success depends on skill, on the perfection of the mental organization, is comparatively modern; it may not be older than the Greeks. A considerable part of the world still believes that success depends on the help of external powers, gods, demons, or whatever it may be. In order to succeed, therefore, it is most important that the artisan should propitiate those powers. Thus the coolies at a salt factory "never scrape salt from the pans without making a Gaṇeśa [the elephant headed god, remover of obstacles] of a small heap of salt." The principal object of worship of certain washermen of Mysore is "the pot of boiling water in which dirty clothes are steeped. Animals are sacrificed to the god with a view to preventing the clothes being burnt in the pot." Certain fishermen on a certain day worship the fishing basket and the trident.[39] Businessmen worship their books once a year, and a friend of mine has seen a dancing girl worship her anklets.

The priestly character of all craftsmen may explain why the Sinhalese smith of the seventeenth century would sit solemnly on a stool, content to hold the iron, and give it now and again a finishing touch, while the customer did the work:[40] he was not so much the man who did the forging as the master of those ceremonies that ensured success in forging. Crafts and rites are not strictly distinguishable, and the Sanskrit word *karma,* "deed," "work," expresses both. The craftsman is, as it were, the man who has the ear of the deity presiding over some particular activity. Heredity is an important, though not the only, qualification for this relation to the deity.

IV

The conclusion we have arrived at on modern evidence is that the caste system is a sacrificial organization, that the aristocracy are feudal lords constantly involved in rites for which they require vassals or serfs, because some of these services involve pollution from which the lord must remain free.

How far is this conception ancient?

The idea of service is contained in the writings that follow the Vedic period. They are agreed that the royal caste was created for justice, for the protection of the people, and so for war and executive power; the priests for ritual and study; the farmers for cattle-breeding, trade, and cultivation; the serfs for crafts and service.[41]

These texts, like our modern witnesses, do not, as a rule, give any hint as to the nature of those services, for the excellent reason that they were addressing themselves to an audience to which these services were quite familiar. Books do not set out to tell what everybody knows. Nevertheless, the *Viṣṇu Purāṇa* does definitely state the ritual character of caste. It says that Brahmā made this entire fourfold system for the performance of the sacrifice. A practical demonstration of this thesis is given us at the present day by certain castes of South India, the subdivisions of which are called *bali,* sacrifice; each subdivision is thus a group with common rites, or, as we might put it, a group the members of which are in communion with one another.[42]

The sacrificial basis of caste appears still more clearly when we go further back to the old ritual literature. There the worthy or excellent castes are those which alone are admitted to share in the sacrifice, with whom alone the gods hold converse.[43] We must not take this to mean that the craftsmen have no religion, or that they have a different religion from the aristocratic castes. Formulae exist for placing the sacrificial fire of the chariot-maker.[44] But the ritual books are not concerned with religion in general and the rites of all classes, but mainly with the state sacrifices, such as the king's consecration, the priest's installation, and so forth. The main object of these sacrifices was the pursuit of immortality; not immortality as we understand it, but freedom from premature death and the diseases that cause it and the renewal of this vigorous life hereafter. "This is the immortality of man," says one authority, "that he reaches a complete life." And again, "Immortality endless, unbounded, is as much as a hundred years."[45] It is a very concrete and immediate immortality. It is to be secured by becoming a god and ascending to the world of the gods. In the words of the teacher, "The sacrificer passes from men to the gods." The way in which this is effected is explained thus: "The sacrifice is the other self of the gods; . . . therefore the sacrificer having made the sacrifice, his other self takes his place in this sky, this heavenly world."[46] In other words, the process is:

$$\begin{aligned} \text{sacrifice} &= \text{gods;} \\ \text{sacrificer becomes} &= \text{sacrifice;} \\ \therefore\ \text{sacrificer becomes} &= \text{gods.} \end{aligned}$$

As vehicles of the immortal gods (immortal in the sense of possessing the full life) the members of the three excellent castes may not come into contact with death and that which leads to death, namely decay and disease. Such a contact would impair their full life, on which the life of the community depends.

If one section may not concern itself with the inauspicious ritual of death for fear of contaminating the auspicious ritual of life, then some other section must handle death and decay, for these are inexorable facts and must be dealt with. A hereditary group, therefore, is necessary to deal with them. These men are the serfs, the *śūdras* of later writings, the *dasyu* or *dāsa* of the *Rigveda*. They are not in communion with the gods; they were not created simultaneously with the gods like the higher castes;[47] on the contrary, they are demons, *asura*, the powers of darkness.[48]

It seems monstrous to the modern mind that a whole section of the community should be identified with the powers of evil; therefore the modern mind refuses to take such statements seriously. "Mere priestly arrogance," it is said. But we have seen at the present day Sinhalese drummers, serfs of the "good people," impersonating demons, and on that account taking no part in the Buddhist ritual which is the heir of the old brahmanic state ritual. It is only natural that those who "are priests on the cremation ground" should be representatives of the powers of darkness and death.

It will be easier for us to admit the literal truth of the statements of early writers if we remember that our word demon is not a satisfactory translation of the words *asura* and *yaksha:* there is too much of wickedness in it. The *asura* are not evil incarnate, like our devils: they are merely the powers of darkness, which are evil only insofar as they encroach too much on light. We should perhaps come nearer the truth if we described *deva* and *asura* as light god and dark god. There is not even a strict line of demarcation, for the sun is called an *asura,* just as Apollo is called a Titan.[49] Perhaps we might speak of "gods" and "titans": it would be historically correct, for the Titans of the Greeks and the *asura* of the Indians are certainly derived from a common stem. A god may be partly a titan; Soma, for instance, who is also Vṛtra.[50] In the same way the human representatives of titans can also represent gods: thus the serfs are identified with titans, but also with the god Pūṣan, "the kinsman of heaven and earth."[51] They represent gods in certain episodes of the ritual. In the king's consecration, certain court officials belonging to the fourth caste (for serfdom is not inconsistent with important office near the king) take a walk-on part, as it were; they do so as gods, even such great gods as Rudra. And yet, even though they stand for gods, their presence causes the king "to enter darkness," as the sun "stricken with darkness" by the demon "does not shine." The king, therefore, has to offer a pap to the gods Soma and Rudra that they may "repel that darkness of his."[52]

V

In conclusion, castes are merely families to whom various offices in the ritual are assigned by heredity.

That is merely the theory which the ancient texts have dinned into the deaf ears of nineteenth–century scholars. Bred with a rationalistic, anti-priestly bias, these scholars consistently have rejected this theory as nothing but an invention of the priests in order to spread their tentacles through the social fabric. We, however, have seen the theory held quite as strongly by peasants and others quite free from all priestly taint. It is a popular view of caste.

We can now take up our ancient texts with greater confidence in their veracity.

Rigveda x, 90 expresses this theory by making caste proceed from the sacrifice. It is curious that this formulation should have been treated as fantastic theology, when Manu has told us very clearly in what sense the castes are born of the ritual. He has shown us every youth of good family going through the ritual of initiation, as the result of which he is reborn as a member of his father's caste. This is not fantastic theology, but a common process found all over the world and not confined to India. Every son of a brahman is born of his father, but he is also born of the sacrifice, and so is every kṣatriya and every farmer. Hence such expressions as "the first-born of prayer" (Rgv., III, 29, 15), "twice-born, first-born of the ritual" (Rgv., x, 61, 19; cp. II, 144, 17; I, 164, 37).

This type of myth is not confined to the priests. Telugu bangle-makers believe that their caste is born of the sacrifice, and therefore they call themselves *Balija,* "Born of the Offering." They describe this birth in the following manner: "Pārvatī was not satisfied with her appearance when she saw herself in the looking-glass, and asked her father to tell her how she was to make herself more attractive. He accordingly prayed to Brahmā, who ordered him to perform a severe penance. From the sacrificial fire kindled in connection therewith arose a being leading a donkey laden with heaps of bangles, turmeric, palm leaf rolls for ears, black beads, sandal powder, a comb, perfumes, etc. To this Great Man (*mahāpuruṣa*) in token of respect were given flags, torches, and certain musical instruments."[53]

Such a myth invariably is rejected as historically worthless because it is physically impossible. It is not so. Causing men to pass through fire, scorching them on a heap of brushwood, and other forms of fictitious cremation are an essential episode of many initiation ceremonies which cause a man to be reborn.[54] It is perfectly possible then for a man to be reborn as bangle-maker as the result of passing through fire. If it appears impossible to us, that is due to our ignorance: we may know physics, but we do not know the customs of the world.

The evidence of *Rigveda,* x, 90 often is brushed aside on the ground that it is a late hymn; but the *argumentum a silentio* is a dangerous one: the first appearance of a custom in the texts is seldom, if ever, its first appearance in the world. It often is not recorded until it begins to decay. In this case there is not even silence: we have quoted from earlier books to show that the idea of rebirth from the sacrifice existed before book x.

How much older? India alone can never answer that question: it will take us back as far as the *Rigveda* and leave us there. If we wish to get beyond, we must resort to comparative evidence, as did the philologists when they wanted to get back beyond the dialects of the Vedas and of Homer to the parent tongue.[55]

The comparative evidence lies outside the scope of this paper: I hope to deal with it exhaustively in some other papers. In the meantime I can only anticipate it by warning the reader that myths of the type of *Rigveda,* x, 90, are not confined to India. They are worldwide. They mostly describe the creation of the world and man in general, but sometimes they account for the divisions of the people, somewhat on the lines of the Viṣṇu Purāṇa, I, 6, 6, and of Manu, I, 87 ff.,[56] only in a more matter of fact way, since they are popular, not learned, versions. The gist of them is that the ancestor, the god, at his installation assigns to each branch of his family in the order of seniority the duties it will have to perform in the state ceremonial.[57]

We are faced with two alternatives: either all these myths were derived from India after the composition of the Puruṣa hymn, or else that hymn is merely the Indian version of a much older myth, older than the Aryan culture of India. The first alternative does not appear to fit the facts, so we are left with the second.

To return to India, our next task is to show that the details of its caste system fit in perfectly well with the theory which makes it an organization for ritual, that the alleged inconsistencies are misunderstandings on our part, misunderstandings which spring, like our disbelief in the legend of the *Balija,* from our ignorance of living institutions; for when we examine these we shall find that they fully corroborate the ancient texts, and that India has not changed as much as is often supposed.

8

Many-armed Gods

Prof. A. A. Macdonell has expounded, in the *Festschrift Ernst Windisch,* a theory to explain why Hindu images are provided with many arms. I have not access to the original so must base my remarks on the summary which he himself gives in the *Journal of the Royal Asiatic Society* for 1916.

His theory is that an additional pair of arms was added by sculptors to carry the attributes which enabled the worshipper to identify the god. The original pair of hands was engaged in the action of blessing, or teaching, or whatever it was the god might be doing, and so could not hold anything.

The theory has merits which are wanting in too many theories of religion or art: it assigns a very precise cause and seeks to derive the effects in a natural manner without resorting to a subsidiary hypothesis or taking refuge in the capriciousness of things. Nevertheless, I think that most of us do not feel quite satisfied. Even without analyzing the facts one has a vague feeling that it is not compelling, because it does not quite fit all the facts. When we come to analyze, we realize the following difficulties.

(1) It seems a very roundabout way of solving the problem to add a pair of arms. Earlier art solved it quite simply by giving the clue on the

Acta Orientalia, vol. 7, 1929, pp. 91–6.

pedestal.[1] The Hindu artist sometimes neglects to make use of the two arms: thus in an image of Brahmā at Kūmbakonam and a Vaikuṇṭha at Manakkai the attributes are represented above the extra hands and not in contact with them.[2]

(2) Some statues have several heads. This peculiarity is as much absent from early art as the many pairs of arms, and it is natural, therefore, to seek for the cause of its later appearance in the same direction.

(3) Some statues have more than two pairs of arms, although none of them hold any attributes; for instance, the Nārāyaṇa at Deogarh, where the hands are not wanted for any particular action and could easily have held attributes.[3] This is quite an early example, too, belonging to the Gupta period. Indeed, on reviewing the history of Hindu sculpture one gains the impression that the obligatory bearing of attributes is late. In the earlier sculptures the arms are performing all kinds of actions with empty hands, or with weapons that are not distinctive, e.g., the Dancing Śiva and the Bhairava at Ellora, Vishṇu of the Three Steps at Seven Pagodas, and so forth. In all these bas-reliefs the multiplication of arms denotes superhuman power and activity. In course of time narrative sculpture disappears, according to the inevitable tendency of the Indian mind, the figures become set, the arms cease to move, and it is then that they are used as convenient attribute-holders.

(4) The presence or absence of extra arms is subject to definite rules. Thus Vishṇu as Vishṇu and in certain of his incarnations has four arms, but as Rāma he should never have more than two. As Balarāma he may have two or four: if two, he carries two attributes; if four, four, which shows that the number of attributes depends on the number of arms and not vice versa. The Candraśekhara aspect of Śiva has four arms when in a pacific mood, eight in one not specified by our authority, ten when killing Gajāsura, but apparently never six.[4] Goddesses carry attributes, yet have only two arms, except Kālī.

Evidently theological considerations were paramount in deciding the number of arms, and this is far more in accord with what we know of the Indian mind than is Prof. Macdonell's theory. Technical considerations carry far less weight with the Indian than with us.

The idea of beings with more than one head and two arms is as old as Indian literature. Prof. Macdonell has himself quoted passages from the *Rigveda* attributing to the gods many faces and limbs. Puruṣa was thousand-headed, thousand-eyed, thousand-footed. Buddhist legend describes Māra making himself thousand-armed for his assault on the Buddha, yet Buddhist sculpture makes no attempt to suggest this.[5]

The idea is older even than Indian literature, since it is found in other countries where it can scarcely have been borrowed from India. The Romans gave Janus two faces. Homer knew that Skylla had many heads.

Cerberus had three. Geryon was reputed to have had three heads, and his dog had two. The Greeks were not content to imagine this, but attempted to translate their fantasies into art; they drew Geryon as three men joined together like Siamese twins, or as one pair of legs carrying a triple torso.[6]

Long before that, Egyptian artists had represented the sun disk with many hands, some holding symbols, some held out to protect the king.[7]

Neither in Egypt nor in Greece did these experiments take root. In Egypt they were made under the influence of an Asiatic heresy, and in Greece when art was still a minor interest, not yet emancipated from pre-Greek and Asiatic art. The artistic sense of both nations rejected these monstrosities. Buddhist art was a pupil of the Greeks and Persians. The influence of its teachers was confirmed by its own sense of moderation, its aversion for violence, extravagance, and profusion. The breakdown of this restraint allowed the conceptions which it had moderated in literature and suppressed altogether in art to display themselves with an insolence born of long repression.

This outbreak may have no lineal connection with the early experiments of the Greeks and Egyptians. Literature alone may have preserved the tradition of many heads and numerous arms, but it is also possible that there was a continuous artistic tradition, notwithstanding the apparent gap of many centuries between the last Greek and the earliest Hindu multi-armed beings. Archaeologists are somewhat too much inclined to confine their attention to the art of the schools. In Europe there is little harm done, at least during those periods when society is fairly homogeneous, because all classes accept the lead of the schools, and those who cannot attain to that standard abstain from art. It is very different in India, where the distance between the highest and lowest is so great, and exclusiveness is so intense that the best people scorn to know what the lowest do, and the lowest have little opportunity of observing what the best do, and so must fall back to a great extent on their own resources. Thus there is in India, besides the standard art, what we may call the coolies' art, which shows no trace of the influence of schools. That art, which uses lime and red dust, would delight the prehistoric archaeologist if found in the course of excavations, but as they are freshly drawn on modern cooly lines or in caves they are unduly despised and their moral is not appreciated. Their moral is that there may be a popular art in perishable materials side by side with the rich man's more refined and durable art, which alone survives for the archaeologist. Another form of popular and perishable art which the more cultivated would disown is masks. These also owe very little to the higher art: they can owe very little because they cultivate the grotesque, which the schools generally avoid. The Siṃhalese poem *Yakkun Natanava,* translated by John Callaway (p. 3), has a verse (no. 16): "A mask was fastened to his head in order to make sixteen faces like those of a tiger and a deer." Now the use of masks goes back to a remote antiquity. Some of the characteristics of Siṃhalese masks, such as the big eye teeth and the bulging eyes, are also found in Javanese masks. They must then have a pretty ancient history, though they never appear in the art of the schools, or only in a very chastened form. Compare, for instance, the Javanese demons of Boro-Budur[8] with Javanese masks. After all, it is not usual to see the devil with cloven feet, tail, and horns at the Royal Academy, though he occurs in comical and superstitious prints. In another thousand years there may not be a single devil extant, but plenty of marble statues inspired by Greece.

The Siṃhalese potters have a plastic art which is so independent of sculpture that it may very well be a continuation of prehistoric models.[9]

Thus there are plenty of ways in which an artistic tradition may continue underground till the decadence of the leaders of thought and art allows it to emerge.

We have definite evidence that many-armed gods were incubating for centuries before they were manifested in sculpture. Śiva appears with four arms on coins of Kaniṣka and Huviṣka in the first century of our era at the very time when the Gandhāra school was Hellenizing Indian art, i.e., introducing Greek ideal types.[10] It is only the accident of his appearing on these coins that has preserved for us the fact that such figures existed side by side with the higher art, and it may be mere accident that no record is preserved of their still earlier appearance.

In order to understand how these monstrosities ultimately gained access into the higher art, we must study similar processes among ourselves. Until no very distant epoch there was only one kind of music heard in Western Europe: there were varieties of that music, from the commonplace easily understood by the masses to the classical understood only by the more musical and better trained minds, but it was at bottom the same music, the popular imitating the classical, *longo intervallo*. In recent times, however, the leaders have lost control, the masses have rebelled and sought their inspiration in negro and other barbaric music, and have produced a style which defiantly sets out to shock all accepted canons of taste. At first jazz was confined to the low dancing hall, but it eventually forced its way into the best drawing rooms, and no one will dance to anything else. It has not, however, yet penetrated, thank God, the concert hall. Thus we have two musics side by side which eventually may fuse, one by discarding vulgarity, the other restraint.

I conceive that something similar happened in India. Monstrosity was just one symptom of the revolt against the intellectuals. At Ellora it is still breathing defiance at the more sober Buddhist art beside it. A few centuries later its innovations were universally accepted, and degenerated into the stale and tasteless commonplaces which suggested to Prof. Macdonell his theory.

It remains to trace the history of this type before its recognition by the schools. In order to trace it satisfactorily we may have to extend our inquiry beyond the confines of India, for India, like every other country, is part of a whole and interacts with the other parts. I should like to draw attention to the three-headed and four-armed Ethiopian deity illustrated in the English translation of Prof. Erman's *Handbook of Egyptian Religion*. Mrs. C. W. H. Johns, the translator, and Prof. F. D. Griffith have kindly answered my inquiries thus: "The representation of the composite deity is unique in Nubia and unparalleled in Egypt. It is on a Meroitic temple at Naga, the date of which is now ascertained to be late in the first, or more probably in the first half of the second, century A.D. It can hardly be later or earlier than that. The god is named Aperėmak and is elsewhere figured with one lion-head."[11] The figure is thus nearly contemporary with Kaniṣka and Huviṣka. Since it is a solitary example, it can scarcely be the original of the four-armed Śiva. The artist may have imitated Indian models; possibly the movement may have started in a third quarter, taken root in India, but perished in Nubia.

The main problem, however, is not so much how the conception got into art, as how it got into the human mind. The many-handed sun-disc of Akuenaten may possibly be a clue.

9

Rotation

Dr. Th. Hugo Horwitz in two articles on rotation[1] has made an important contribution to the evolution of the wheel and other rotating machines. It is important because he has realized that in order to make progress we must study not isolated contrivances, but the principles underlying them all. We shall never get far if we are content to study the potter's wheel only, or the chariot wheel only, or the spindle only; we must take rotation as the object of our study and take into account all the contrivances in which it may be exemplified.

In that excellent paper I seem to detect one inconsistency. At the outset the author distinguishes lower rotary technique, in which there are no fixed bearings, e.g., a roller, and higher rotary technique, in which there are fixed bearings as in the carriage wheel (p. 726). At the end he tells us the higher technique occurs only in Eurasia (120), yet in between he gives two illustrations of what appears to be the higher technique in South America: women use as fixed bearing for one end of the spindle either the interval between big toe and second toe, or else a forked piece of wood.

The higher technique has then reached America. What is true is that it has not developed there. Why? Because the possibility of utilizing the momentum evidently has not occurred. The spindle turns only as long as the thread is pulled. Now momentum is used in the lower technique, as in

Anthropos, vol. 29, 1934, p. 812.

tops (which our author overlooks) and in balls. Fixed bearings increase the friction and so destroy one great asset of round bodies, namely momentum. Take that away and there is not much point in roundness. The only advantage of a fixed bearing in South American spinning is to release one hand.

Until the friction with the bearings can be so reduced that the shaft goes on turning, there is no great incentive to make use of the higher technique. Lubrication solves the problem, so at this point the history of rotation becomes intertwined with that of lubrication. Yet lubrication has been entirely neglected by technologists. Let us hope that Dr. Horwitz will help to fill the gap.

He will, however, find himself much hampered so long as he persists in drawing a hard and fast line between technology and ritual. He roundly declares that a technical discovery cannot arise out of ritual-mythological conceptions. No instance, he says, has ever been produced. Is it not because this dogma has prevented people from seeing cases? I do not know if Dr. Horwitz will accept a surgical operation as "technical." If he does, he must admit that the technical operation of removing the foreskin for hygienic reasons has been imitated by many Christians from the Jewish circumcision, which is purely "ritual-mythological." I have pointed out in my *Progress of Man*[2] that ritual anointing with oil and rubbing with fat is much more ancient than "technical" lubrication. Men who have no idea of lubrication are, in consequence, well acquainted with the slippery properties of fat and oil. It is quite arbitrary to assert that the experience gained when anointing an image or a candidate has played no part in the discovery of lubrication. In the same way it seems quite arbitrary to deny, as Dr. Horwitz does, that experience of rotation in the course of ritual is never utilized in mechanical processes. Man's mind is not thus divided into watertight compartments.

Notes

Editor's Introduction

1. For a longer account of his life, together with an estimation of his work, see the reissue of Hocart's *Kings and Councillors*, ed. and intr. Rodney Needham (Chicago: University of Chicago Press, 1970), editor's introduction: see also the editor's entry on Hocart in the *International Encyclopedia of the Social Sciences* 18—*Biographical Supplement* (New York: Free Press, 1979): 305–7. His publications are listed in Rodney Needham, *A Bibliography of Arthur Maurice Hocart* (Oxford: Basil Blackwell, 1967); additions and corrections are reported, under the heading "Hocart Bibliography," in Needham, *Man*, N.S. 4 (1969): 292; Kitsiri Malalgoda, *Man* 11 (1976): 439–40; and William Logan, *Man* 17 (1982): 778–9.

2. *Caste: A Comparative Study* (London: Methuen, 1950).

3. London: Methuen, 1952.

4. Occasional Papers of the Royal Anthropological Institute 11 (London: Royal Anthropological Institute, 1952).

5. London: Watts, 1954.

6. For references, see *Kings and Councillors*, 2d ed., pp. xv–xvi.

7. Meyer Fortes, "On Installation Ceremonies," *Proceedings of the Royal Anthropological Institute*, 1967: 5–19 (esp. pp. 5, 19).

8. New York: Russell & Russell.

9. London: Oxford University Press.

10. 2d impr., ed. with a foreword by Rodney Needham (London: Methuen).

11. In the series "Classics in Anthropology," published by the University of Chicago Press.

12. *Kingship* (London: Oxford University Press, 1927), p. 159.

13. First published as *Les Castes* (Paris: Musée Guimet, 1938); English edition, *Caste* (London: Methuen, 1950).

14. Louis Dumont, *La Civilisation indienne et nous* (Paris: Colin, 1964), pp. 90–97, 108; *Homo hierarchicus: essai sur le régime des castes* (Paris: Gallimard, 1966), see index, p. 422, under "Hocart."

15. [D. F. Pocock], "A. M. Hocart on Caste—Religion and Power," *Contributions to Indian Sociology* 2 (1958): 45–63.

16. The essay has been reproduced, as the first third of the chapter on India, in *Caste* (London: Methuen, 1952), pp. 1–23.

17. [Subtitle]: *A Short Survey of his Evolution, his Customs and his Works* (London: Methuen, 1933), pp. 233–4.

18. I. M. Lewis, "Problems in the Comparative Study of Unilineal Descent," in Michael Banton, ed., *The Relevance of Models for Social Anthropology,* A.S.A. Monographs 1 (London: Tavistock Publications, 1965), p. 106.

19. Rodney Needham, "Remarks on the Analysis of Kinship and Marriage," in idem *Remarks and Inventions: Skeptical Essays about Kinship* (London: Tavistock Publications; New York: Harper & Row, 1974), chap. 1.

20. Rodney Needham, "The Evolution of Social Classification: A Commentary on the Warao Case," *Bijdragen tot de Taal-, Land- en Volkenkunde* 130 (1974), pp. 16–43.

21. Emile Durkheim, *Les Règles de la méthode sociologique* (Paris, 1895), esp. chap. 4: "Règles relatives à l'explication des faits sociaux."

22. G. C. Homans and D. M. Schneider, *Marriage, Authority and Final Causes* (Glencoe, Illinois: Free Press, 1955); repr. in G. C. Homans, *Sentiments and Activities: Essays in Social Science* (New York: Free Press of Glencoe, 1962), chap. 14.

23. Rodney Needham, *Structure and Sentiment* (Chicago: University of Chicago Press, 1962; 4th impr. cor., 1969).

24. Cf. A. L. Kroeber, "Disposal of the Dead" (*American Anthropologist* 29 [1927]: 308–15), p. 313: "the immediacy and intensity of an emotion concerning a cultural practice are no index of the origin or durability of that practice."

25. *The Life-giving Myth,* pp. 39–45.

26. C. Lévi-Strauss, "The Structural Study of Myth," in Thomas A. Sebeok, ed., *Myth: A Symposium* (Philadelphia: American Folklore Society, 1955), pp. 50–75 (see p. 57). Actually, the point was made long before Lévi-Strauss, as he was to acknowledge, by Vladimir Propp, in *Morphology of the Folktale,* original Russian ed., 1928; English ed., trans. L. Scott, *International Journal of American Linguistics* 24 (1958); cf. Lévi-Strauss, "La Structure et la forme: réflexions sur un ouvrage de Vladimir Propp," *Cahiers de l'Institut de Science Economique appliquée,* No. 99 (1960): 3–36 (see p. 16).

27. Berthold Delbrück, "Die indogermanischen Verwandtschaftsnamen: ein Beitrag zur vergleichenden Alterthumskunde," *Abhandlungen der Philologisch-Historischen Klasse der Königlich Sächsischen Gesellschaft der Wissenschaften* 11 (1889): 379–606.

28. Hocart, writing in Ceylon, seems not to have been acquainted with Schrader's important researches into Indo-European terms of affinity: O. Schrader, "Ueber Bezeichnungen der Heiratsverwandtschaft bei den idg. Völkern," *Indogermanische Forschungen* 17 (1904): 11–36.

29. See Rodney Needham, "Prescription," *Oceania* 43 (1973): 166–81.

30. Robert H. Lowie, "Relationship Terms," *Encyclopaedia Britannica,* 14th ed. (1929), s.v.

31. Rodney Needham, "An Analytical Note on the Structure of Sirionó So-

ciety," *Southwestern Journal of Anthropology* 17 (1961): 239–55; see the reference to "the usual feature of [prescriptive] alliance systems" to the effect that in the Sirionó classification there are no special affinal terms (p. 244). Cf. Louis Dumont, *Introduction à deux théories d'anthropologie sociale* (Paris: Mouton, 1971), p. 114: "Le trait général, et caractéristique, des vocabulaires correspondant au mariage des cousins croisés est l'absence de termes distincts pour les parents par affinité."

32. A. M. Hocart, *Lau Islands, Fiji,* Bernice P. Bishop Museum Bulletin 62 (Honolulu, 1929), p. 33. Cf., e.g., Rodney Needham, "Terminology and Alliance, I: Garo, Manggarai," *Sociologus* 16 (1966): 141–57 (see p. 145, table 1; p. 151, table 2); idem, "Endeh: Terminology, Alliance, and Analysis," *Bijdragen tot de Taal-, Land- en Volkenkunde* 124 (1968): 305–35 (see p. 315, table 2).

33. Louis Dumont, "The Dravidian Kinship Terminology as an Expression of Marriage," *Man* 53 (1953): 34–9, art. 54 (see p. 38).

34. "Proto-Indo-European Kinship," *Ethnology* 5 (1966): 1–36.

35. Friedrich, p. 25.

36. Friedrich, p. 29. For criticism of the substantive label "Omaha," see Rodney Needham, "Gurage Social Classification: Formal Notes on an Unusual System," *Africa* 39 (1969): 153–66; idem, *Remarks and Inventions* (London: Tavistock Publications; New York: Harper & Row, 1974), chap. 1.

37. "Proto-Indo-European Kinship," p. 29. (By a misprint, incidentally, Hocart's argument appears at first to be placed in an earlier essay on the cousin in Vedic ritual [1925], instead of in his essay on Indo-European Kinship.)

38. *Vocabulaire des institutions indo-européennes,* 2 vols. (Paris: Editions de Minuit, 1969), vol. 1: *Économie, parenté, société,* bk. 2 (pp. 203–76).

39. On the latter count, it should perhaps be mentioned that Jack Goody has published a paper, "Indo-European Kinship," on the patrilineal character ascribed to Indo-European society (*Comparative Studies in Kinship* [London: Routledge & Kegan Paul, 1969], chap. 9). He writes, however, without reference to Delbrück, Schrader, or Hocart (to cite no more of the standard scholarly sources on this well-established theme), and his views are thereby inevitably much weakened.

40. His argument calls for a detailed analysis too extensive to find room here.

41. Though the "Seneca-Iroquois" of North America should not actually be included. The "trifling modification" to which Hocart alludes is a systematic terminological difference that removes this society from the class of prescriptive systems.

42. Cf. Rodney Needham, ed., *Right and Left: Essays on Dual Symbolic Classification* (Chicago: University of Chicago Press, 1973).

43. Hocart's essay has been taken up by C. Lévi-Strauss, in *Les Structures élémentaires de la parenté* (Paris: Presses Universitaires de France, 1949), p. 500, but he gets the facts wrong. According to Lévi-Strauss, Buddha married Devadatta, "sa cousine croisée," his female cross-cousin (cf. English ed., *The Elementary Structures of Kinship,* ed. Rodney Needham, trans. J. H. Bell, J. R. von Sturmer, and R. Needham [Boston: Beacon Press, 1969], p. 403). As Rajah Wijetunge comments, "Whether Devadatta was Prince Siddharta's cross-cousin as given in the southern interpretation or a parallel cousin as represented by the northern tradition, he remains (as is widely and commonly known) a male" (letter: "Prince Siddharta's Cross-Cousin," *Man* n.s. 7 [1972]: 138). Wijetunge raises the possibility that Lévi-Strauss got his inaccuracy from M. B. Emeneau's "Was There Cross-Cousin Marriage Among the Śākyas?" (*Journal of the American Oriental Society* 59 [1939]: 220–6), which he also cites, but Emeneau says no such thing. (See also

Kalipada Mitra, "Cross-Cousin Relation between Buddha and Devadatta," *Indian Antiquary* 53 [1924]: 125–8.) As for the argument itself, however, it should be added that Emeneau thinks it unwarranted: "Not only is there no evidence for such a joking-relationship elsewhere in Buddhist literature, but even the cross-cousin type of kinship between the Buddha and Devadatta is in all probability merely a Sinhalese fabrication and not to be used as the basis for any hypotheses about social conditions in the Buddha's own community" (226).

44. *Festschrift Ernst Windisch* (Leipzig: Harrassowitz, 1914), pp. 158–69.

45. *Journal of the Royal Asiatic Society* (1916): 125–30.

46. Jitendra Nath Banerjea, *The Development of Hindu Iconography,* 2d ed. rev. and enl. (Calcutta: University of Calcutta, 1956), pp. 81–2; cf. p. 305.

Cf. Ananda K. Coomaraswamy, "Indian Images with Many Arms," in idem, *The Dance of Shiva,* rev. ed. (New York: Noonday Press, 1957), pp. 79–84. In Coomaraswamy's assessment of the topic there is expressed an openness of mind wholly reminiscent of Hocart: "To appreciate any art . . . we ought not to concentrate our attention upon its peculiarities—ethical or formal—but should endeavor to *take for granted* whatever the artist takes for granted" (p. 84).

On the theological aspect, see also, e.g., Alain Daniélou, *Hindu Polytheism,* Bollingen Series 73 (New York: Pantheon Books, 1964), p. 216: "The four arms of Śiva are a sign of universal power. They represent the four divisions of space and show mastery over the elements."

47. *The Progress of Man* (1933), pp. 66–7; cf. p. 146.

Chapter 1: Evidence in Human History

1. For Agni see A. A. Macdonell, *Vedic Mythology,* and E. W. Hopkins, *Epic Mythology,* both in G. Buhler's *Grundriss der Indo-Germanischen Philologie,* III.—*Śatapatha Brāhmana* (*S.B.*), VIII, 6, 6; VI, 4, 4, 11; 5, 1, 12; V, 3, 2, 1, 1; III, 2, 2, 12; et passim—*Rigveda* (*Rgv.*), I, 1; X, 16.

For Hermes: Daremberg et Saglio, *Dictionnaire d'antiquités grecques et latines,* s.v. Mercurius.—Hesiod, *Theogony,* 939; *Op.* 80.—*Homeric Hymn* (*H.H.*), IV.—Pausanias, IX, 22, 1; V, 27, 8; IV, 3, 3, 4; VI, 26, 5; II, 3, 4.—L. R. Farnell, *Cults of the Greek States,* V, 22.

2. T. W. Rhys Davids, *Buddhism,* pp. 115ff.

Chapter 2: The Convergence of Customs

1. Fletcher, *A History of Architecture,* pp. 337, 347.

2. Foucher, *L'Art gréco-bouddhique du Gandhara,* vol. I.

3. Fletcher, op. cit. Fig. 256 and p. 629; Fergusson, *A History of Indian and Eastern Architecture* (1910), vol. I, p. 317.

4. "Early Fijians," *Journal of the Anthropological Institute,* 1919, p. 42.

5. Vol. xi, 1912, p. 85.

6. "Spirit Animals," *Man,* 1915, pp. 147–50, art. 86.

7. "Fiji: Totemism," *Man,* 1910, no. 12.

8. For convergence in zoology see *Les Vertébrés vivants et fossiles* (Musée Royal d'Histoire Naturelle, Brussels). I here take the opportunity of thanking the author, Mr. Louis Dollo, for his great courtesy and indefatigable zeal in demon-

strating his collections, and thereby helping me to realize more clearly than I had theretofore the true nature of convergence.

Chapter 3: Psychology and Ethnology

1. People are not yet agreed whether to speak of Indo-Germanic or Indo-European languages, and no one is quite satisfied with either.

2. Frazer, *Totemism and Exogamy,* vol. iv, p. 106.

3. Frazer, *Totemism and Exogamy,* vol. iv, p. 105.

4. ibid., p. 113.

5. *Reports of the Cambridge Expedition to Torres Straits,* vol. v, p. 222 ff.

6. Most theories of marriage seem to assume that it is based on the sexual instinct and jealousy. If it is so, it is hard to understand why those people who allow premarital freedom and do not enforce conjugal fidelity should marry at all. In certain parts of the world marriage looks more like an economic institution; premarital intrigues are love affairs, but marriage is business. Love as the real or ostensible motive possibly is limited to a minority of races, and due to the almost impossibility of indulging romance outside of marriage and to a strict individualism that makes pleasant companionship the all-important consideration in marriage.

7. "A Native Fijian on the Decline of his Race," *Hibbert Journal,* vol. xi, 1912–13, p. 35.

8. Poincaré, *Science et hypothèse,* p. 170.

9. Poincaré, op. cit., p. 119.

10. ibid., p. 66.

11. *Hibbert Journal,* l.c.

12. With apologies to *Notes and Queries of the British Association,* p. 252.

13. With apologies to Mr. Carveth Read, "The Conditions of Belief in Immature Minds," *British Journal of Psychology,* vol. vi, pp. 314, 315.

14. Nor must Kohler be forgotten, whose monograph *Zur Urgeschichte der Ehe* [Stuttgart, 1895] will delight all those who enjoy mathematical precision. [English edition, trans. R. H. Barnes and Ruth Barnes, ed. and intr. R. H. Barnes, *On the Prehistory of Marriage* (Classics in Anthropology), Chicago and London: University of Chicago Press, 1975.]

15. Poincaré, op. cit., p. 211.

Chapter 4: Myths in the Making

1. *American Anthropologist,* vol. xviii, 1916, pp. 57–71. [Repr. in Hocart, *The Life-giving Myth,* ed. Lord Raglan (London: Methuen, 1952); 2d impr., ed. with foreword by Rodney Needham, London: Methuen, 1970.]

2. Athenaeus, 39a: *τὸ ωέκταρ ἐσθίω πάνυ*
μάττων διαπίνω τ' αμβροσίαν.

3. *ἀμβροσίας μέν*
κρατὴρ ἐκέκρατο
Ερμᾶς δ' ἕλεν ὄλπιν
θεοῖς οἰνοχοῆσαι.

4. *Sanskrit Literature,* p. 98.

5. "Chieftainship in the Pacific," *American Anthropologist,* vol. xvii, 1915, p. 631.

6. Dubois, *Hindu Manners and Customs* (Oxford, 1897), vol. i, p. 103.

7. ibid., pp. 239, 246; 225.

8. *Il.* 14, 170, ἀμβροσίῃ μὲν πρῶτον ἀπὸ χροὸς ἱμερόεντος λύματα πάντα κάθηρεν.

9. Or "the *tuka* heresy," as Mr. Basil Thomson calls it (*The Fijians,* p. 140).

10. ibid., p. 133.

11. Giles, *Manual of Comparative Philology,* p. 57.

12. pp. 30–34.

13. Foucher, *Beginnings of Buddhist Art,* Plate ID.

14. Cf. Dubois, op. cit., p. 590; H. Junker, *Die Stundenwachen in den Osirienmysterien* (Virma), p. 6.

*["Some Experiments on the Reproduction of Folk-stories," *Folk-lore,* vol. 31 (1920), pp. 30–47.]

Chapter 5: The Indo-European Kinship System

1. I am much indebted to Mr. S. Paranavitane, my Epigraphical Assistant, for his assistance in compiling this list of Sinhalese terms.

2. "Etymologie des Sinhalesischen," in *Abhandlungen der K. bayer. Akad. der Wiss.,* I cl., XXI, Bd. II, Abth., p. 43.

3. *Epigraphia Zeylanica,* I, 59, no. 6.

4. I am much indebted to Mr. C. Venacitamby, Chief Clerk of the Archaeological Department, for his assistance in compiling this list.

5. There is a variant in the Vinaya Vinicchaya, a compendium of the Vinaya Pitaka. *Mātucchā* is there used for *mātulāni.*

6. The Pali Text Society's Dictionary, s.v. *pitā* takes the terms to mean grandfather and real father, but in Jātaka I, 115, which it quotes, *cullapitar* is not the father.

7. *Commentary on the Dhammapada,* ed. Fausböll, p. 241.

8. Jātaka IV, 323, verse 21; *Samyutta* I 86.

9. "Buddha and Devadatta," *Indian Antiquary,* 1923, p. 267.

10. Macdonell and Keith, *Vedic Index.*

11. V. indicates that the words occur in the Vedas, R.V. in the *Rigveda.*

12. cp. Macdonell and Keith, *Vedic Index,* s.v. *māturbhrātra.*

13. Margaret M. Hardie, "The Significance of Greek Personal Names," *Folklore,* 1923, p. 154.

14. "India and the Pacific," *Ceylon Journal of Science,* sec. G, vol. 1, pt. 2, 1925, p. 163 [*The Life-giving Myth,* chap. 29].

15. "The Cousin in Vedic Ritual, *Indian Antiquary,* vol. 54, 1926, p. 16; "Limitations on the Sister's Son's Right in Fiji," *Man,* vol. 26, art. 134.

Note.—For naming after the grandfather in Ceylon see Mr. Paranavitane's note on line 1 of the Ruvanvälisäya Pillar in vol. III of *Epigraphia Zeylanica.*

Chapter 6: Buddha and Devadatta

1. This pedigree is given in *Mahávaṃsa* 11, 15 ff.

2. Richards, "Cross-cousin Marriage in South India," *Man,* vol. 14, 1914, art. 97; Rivers, *The Todas,* p. 484; Morgan, *Systems of Consanguinity,* pl. x ff.

3. *Cambridge Expedition to the Torres Straits,* VI, p. 92.
4. Morgan, op. cit., pl. IV ff.
5. "The Fijian Custom of *tauvu,*" *JRAI,* vol. 43, 1913, pp. 101–8; "More about *tauvu,*" *Man,* vol. 14, 1914, art. 96; "The Uterine Nephew," *Man,* vol. 23, 1923, art. 4.
6. "Chieftainship and the Sister's Son in the Pacific," *American Anthropologist,* vol. 17, 1915, pp. 631–46.
7. "The Common Sense of Myth," *American Anthropologist,* vol. 18, 1916, pp. 307–18 [*The Life-giving Myth,* chap. 4].
8. Rivers, *History of Melanesian Society,* I, p. 22. The author probably took it more seriously than it was meant.
9. Junod, *Life of a South African Tribe,* I, p. 162.
10. It is quite possible that they have the same origin as the Kṣattriyâs and Brâhmans of India.
11. Rivers, *The Todas,* p. 503.
12. ibid., p. 526.
13. *The Melanesians of British New Guinea,* p. 28.
14. A. Werner, "Some Galla Notes," *Man,* vol. 15, 1915, art. 10.
15. Beal, *Buddhist Records of the Western World,* II, 153.
16. *JRAI,* vol. 52, 1922, pp. 71–112, 259–305.
17. "Note on Various Definitions," *Man,* vol. 20, 1920, pp. 21–23, art. 12.

Chapter 7: The Basis of Caste

1. E. Senart, *Les Castes dans l'Inde* (Paris: Leroux, 1896).
2. *rabāna.*
3. *Vel peḍi* as against *vel vidāne.*
4. Manu IV, 2 ff; E. Thurston, *Castes and Tribes of Southern India,* vol. I (1901), p. 344.
5. Usually described by Europeans as the warrior caste; but fighting, as we shall see, is only a derivative. The essence of their function is sovereignty, kingship, hence the names by which they are known in India.
6. Manu IV 61; *Indian Art and Letters,* vol. 1, p. 19.
7. There are now claimants to the rank of merchant, co-equal with the farmers, but their claim is suspect. I do not here notice the Vanni caste (found locally on the edge of the jungle, and admitted by the farmers to be slightly higher in rank), because they are known to be later immigrants from India.
8. For various lists see F. A. Hayley's *Laws and Customs of the Sinhalese* (Colombo, 1922), p. 89 ff.
9. x. 38.
10. For detailed evidence see *Ceylon Journal of Science,* sec. G, vol. 1, p. 66. Add Vinaya IV, 6.
11. Vinaya IV, 6; Aṅguttara I, 162; Jātaka III, 194; Manu IV 79, XII 55, X 51; Mahāvaṃsa X 92; Skt. Dict. s.v. *divākīrti.*
12. *Halagama* and *Vahunpura.*
13. *Näkati minissu,* from Skt. *nakṣatra,* constellation.
14. *Yakkha,* e.g., *Mahavaṃsa,* XXXVI, 88.
15. *Yakbera* and *singāra gahana minissu.*
16. *Yaksayo karaṇa leḍa.*
17. *Bili,* the true Sinhalese for Skt. *bali.*
18. J. Callaway, Yakkun nattanava, p. 10.

19. *Kuḍimakkal.*

20. *Naḍuvar,* literally "dancers," as opposed to the drummers.

21. Arumugam, "Customs and Ceremonies in the Jaffna District," *Ceylon Antiquary,* vol. 2 (1910), 240.

22. Arumugam, "Customs and Ceremonies in the Jaffna District," p. 244.

23. The term is *prāṇopakāri* (compare psychopompos). E. Thurston, *Tribes and Castes of Southern India,* vol. I, p. 41.

24. Thurston, vol. I, p. 171.

25. *Saivakkuru,* Skt. *Śaiva + guru.*

26. Thurston, vol. II, p. 11.

27. See my "Confinement at Puberty," *Man,* vol. 27, 1927, art. 31.

28. *Ancient Ceylon,* pp. 189, 198.

29. *Pūjāri.*

30. *Piḍāri.* Thurston, vol. III, p. 189.

31. Thurston, s.v. *kusavan.*

32. *Ghaṭikaramahābrahma* in Jātaka, I, 69; Majjhimanikāya, II, 45.

33. Śat. Brāhm., VI, 5, 1. Cp. my *Kingship* (London: Oxford University Press, 1927; 2d impr., 1969), pp. 190–91.

34. See my article "Idolatry" in *Encyclopaedia of the Social Sciences,* vol. 7, 1932, pp. 575–7.

35. For more see Thurston, s.v. *ambalavāsi, bhatrāzu,* etc.

36. Jaggery, *hakuru,* is sugar made from a palm. Mr. S. Paranavitana thinks *hakaru,* as caste name, is a false etymology from a derivative of Skt. *sūpakāra,* cook.

37. Hocart, *The Temple of the Tooth at Kandy* (London: Luzac, 1931), chap. III.

38. *Villi, panna, batgama.*

39. Thurston, IV, 191; I, 17; I, 128.

40. Knox's *Ceylon,* p. 67f.

41. Vāyupurana, VII, 168 ff; Bhāgavata Pur., III, 6, 29; Mahābhārata, Śantip., 3406; Viṣṇu Pur., I, 36; Jātaka, III, 208; Manu, I, 88.

42. Viṣṇu Pur., I, 6, 6. Thurston, I, 24.

43. Śat. Brāhm., III, 1, 1, 9f.

44. Macdonell and Keith, *Vedic Index,* II, 253 referring to Taitt. Brāh., I, 1, 4, 8.

45. Śat. Brāhm., IX, 5, 1, 10; X, 2, 6, 7. Hence the greeting, "Live a hundred years," Jāt., I, 35. Śat. Brāhm. II, 5, 1, 7; X, 2, 6, 4.

46. Śat. Brāhm. VIII, 6, 1, 10.

47. Taitt. Saṃh. VII, 1, 1, 4 ff.

48. Pañcaviṃśa, V, 5, 17. Taitt. Brāhm., I, 2, 6, 7.

49. Ṛgv., I, 35, 10. *C.,* I, 2342.

50. Śat. Brāhm., III, 4, 3, 13 ff.

51. Śat. Brāhm., XIV, 4, 2, 23; Ṛgv., VI, 58, 4.

52. Śat. Brāhm., V, 3, 2, 2; *Kingship,* 113 ff.

53. Thurston, s.v. *Balija. Mahāpuruṣa* is the sacrificial victim in Ṛgv. X, 90.

54. See my *Kingship,* chap. XII, and my *Progress of Man* (London: Methuen, 1933), pp. 151, 158. Quaritch Wales, "Theory and Ritual Connected with Pregnancy," *Journal of the Royal Anthropological Institute,* 1933, p. 441.

55. See my "Evidence in Human History," *Psyche Annual,* vol. 13, 1933, pp. 80–93 [above, chap. I].

56. Or Śat. Brāhm., II, i, 4, 11: "The creator created the earth and the corresponding brahman caste by saying '*bhūḥ,*' the air and the nobility by saying '*bhuvaḥ,*' the heavens and the farmers by saying 'sky'."

57. Cp. *Kingship,* chap. 16.

Chapter 8: Many-armed Gods

1. Vincent Smith, *History of Indian Art,* pl. XXXVIII, fig. 119.
2. Krishna Sastri, *South Indian Images,* pp. 13, 53.
3. Vincent Smith, loc. cit., pl. XXXV.
4. Gopinatha Rao, *Elements of Hindu Iconography,* I, 189; II, 115, etc.
5. Jātaka, I, 72.
6. Walters, *History of Ancient Pottery,* vol. I, pls. XXIII, XXXVIII; vol. II, p. 195.
7. Breasted, *History of Egypt,* p. 368.
8. Foucher, *L'Art gréco-bouddhique,* II, 579.
9. *Ceylon Journal of Science,* sec. G, I, 1924, p. 10.
10. P. Gardner, *Coins of the Greek and Scythian Kings,* pp. 132, 135.
11. Mrs. Johns refers me to Crowfoot's *The Island of Meroë,* and Griffith, *Meroitic Inscriptions,* pt. I, pls. XVI–XX and p. 54ff.

Chapter 9: Rotation

1. *Anthropos,* vol. 28, 1933, pp. 721–57; vol. 29, 1934, pp. 99–125.
2. London: Methuen, 1933, p. 66.

Index